BECOME A BILINGUAL FAMILY

The Best Method for Raising Bilingual Children, Even If You Only Speak One Language

DANIELA PERIEDA
&
LADONNA ATKINS

COPYRIGHT

Bilingual Family LLC
2900 W Hefner Rd.
Oklahoma City, OK 73120
www.bilingualfamily.us

ISBN 978-0-692-75379-8

ACKNOWLEDGMENTS

We first want to thank our dear families for their love and support during our writing journey. We want to thank the families from Bilingual Family for their support. Their dedication to the program has helped shape the ideas and strategies used in this book. Their children are the souls and stories in which this book was created.

Thank you to Dr. Stephen Krashen for his years of dedication and research contributions to the field of Second Language Acquisition.

Special thanks to Kyle Tanner, Heather Hutto, the Martindale family, the Rubio family, the Evers family, the Rodgers family and the Moore family for their thoughtful feedback, insights and support for this book.

Con amor,

Daniela and LaDonna

CONTENTS

Note to Readers

There are many reasons why we felt the need to write this book. We believe in the beauty and benefits of being bilingual and want to provide the best method. We saw the struggles and frustration as families tried to keep their heritage, or teach their children a second language. We both had our own life journeys that influenced this book.

Daniela:

I'm writing this book as a tribute to my first – and best – language teacher, my mom, Claudia Cardoni. I'm also writing it for all the families at my school, Bilingual Family, and families around the world who want to raise bilingual children.

Soon after opening my school, it became apparent that the children with language support at home were acquiring and producing the language at a much faster pace than the children who lacked this support. This didn't necessarily mean that the parents were native speakers. In fact, the majority of the parents were not native speakers and were not fluent in Spanish. But they had a deep desire to learn the language.

After making this observation, I knew it was my responsibility to help parents use Spanish at home, even if they were not native or fluent speakers. My hope is that, by reading this book and applying this method, you not only will learn a second language, but will develop a powerful relationship with your child!

Con amor,

Daniela

LaDonna:

My career with children began when I was fifteen, working in a child care setting. I was fascinated by the children's conversations, fast-paced learning, and how they engaged in play. I found it easy to play right along with them. I knew working with them would be my career.

I excelled and moved quickly through my college degree programs. Learning about children was my passion and I was thoroughly engaged.

I knew I wanted to research more in the area of child's play. Through my doctorial work, I was introduced to play scholars, advocates, and associations focused on the study of play. Since that time, play has become my main area of advocacy and research.

I have taught infants through adults. Throughout my teaching career, I have always been interested in second language learning, yet did not have success in learning a second language. I tried traditional methods to no avail.

When Daniela, a former college colleague, told me her program was based on play and second-language learning, our collaboration began.

Our Voice

This book has been created by two authors, but is written in one voice. We've collaborated on every detail. Though our expertise fall in different fields, we have joined forces to create a program we are passionate about sharing with families. We have both used the strategies in different contexts and believe it is the best method to help you become a bilingual family.

INTRO

L EARNING A SECOND language is all about relationships. In the context of learning, it is in our communication with others that we learn. This book focuses on the best method for raising bilingual children, even if you only speak one language. Learning a second language does not have to be difficult.

So, why is learning a second language all about relationships? Actually it's very simple. Let's look at how we learned our first language. Chances are your parents did not give you a daily grammar lesson as an infant. They didn't write out a list of words for you to memorize, and they did not constantly correct you when you mispronounced a word. Instead, you learned language through constant repetition and interactions that used vocalizations, gestures and expressions. This provides a clue into the way language should be taught.

There's a powerful reason why you want to raise bilingual children. The benefits of being bilingual are numerous. It might be that you want your child to have better opportunities in the future, you want to preserve their heritage, and /or you want them to be global citizens. Whatever the reason, it's important to understand that YOU play a huge role in making language learning a reality. This is why we created this book for YOU!

No single teacher or program has as much influence on your child as you do. You are your child's first and best teacher. So before we get started, we want to thank you for realizing the power you have in choosing to be a vital part of your child's language-learning journey. This book will provide you with a simple, yet powerful method for raising bilingual children. The book will provide resources and tools to take you on the journey of becoming a bilingual family.

IMPORTANT - *Although the routines, common phrases, and vocabulary examples contained in this book are in Spanish, please know our method and strategies can apply to learning any language.*

In the next chapter, I will share my journey through second-language acquisition both as a language learner and as a language teacher. This journey of trials and tribulations helped me discover *how* children acquire a second language. I now use what I have learned to help children and families become bilingual.

THE SPIRIT OF THE TEACHER

I KNOW EXACTLY what's going through your head. You are probably saying: "I don't have the time to teach my child a second language, especially if I don't speak the language myself." We all seem to have a problem with time and I'm sure even my mom, who took the time to teach me the English language, lacked time as well.

But don't worry; this method will introduce a second language without taking too much time out of your day and without stress. This program builds language learning into what you already are doing during your day. If you're reading this book, raising bilingual children is really important to you and it will continue to be important to you even if you do not take action.

Time will fly by, as it tends to do, and you'll realize that your children are grown up and do not speak a second language. If this is important to you, you need to take action now! If my mom had not taken action, I would not be writing this book.

There are so many opportunities when you are bilingual –not only economic opportunities, but opportunities to influence, make an impact, and create relationships with two worlds. That is a gift your children will cherish for their entire lives.

My Journey as a Learner

I was born and raised in Colombia, and when I was about five years old, my mom – a.k.a. play partner and best friend – decided to choose Saturday as our "English day." Because she was my best friend, playmate, and first teacher, I tried my best to understand everything she was saying. By the same token, she used any means necessary (other than translating) to make her message comprehensible.

My mom would wake me up in English and give me simple commands in order to get me ready for the day. We would make breakfast together and play in English. I mostly replied in Spanish, but somehow my mom knew that it would pay off.

During this time, I attended a bilingual school in Colombia, where the English program was meant to grow over time. When I was in kindergarten, I would only get 15 minutes of English each week; in first grade, that rose to 30 minutes and it increased over time. By the time I was in fourth grade, my entire science class was in English.

Today, I recognize that my school played a significant role in my second-language acquisition, but I remain convinced that the main reason I was excited to learn English was because of my relationship with my mom. I was always excited to share the new things I was learning in school and we made English our secret language – the language we could use to make fun of people on the bus.

When I came to the U.S. at age 10, I quickly realized that, while I understood a lot and was able to communicate, reading and writing had not been addressed in my bilingual school. During my first year in fifth grade, I was put in an English as a Second Language (ESL) class to help with reading and writing. This class was helpful, but the key to my acquisition of English and fluency was yet again relationships. All of my new Oklahoman friends were English speakers and this pushed me to communicate and to learn new phrases. The process was effortless.

It's important to note that, while having English-speaking friends was a benefit, many children who grow up bilingual loose their home language when they enter school because all their friends now speak English. How many people do you know whose parents spoke a second language at home, yet they will comment about how they can understand, but not speak that language? They did not use the second language in a meaningful way, so they lost the ability.

Now let's fast-forward to the college years.

From Language Learner to Language Teacher

In my second year of college, I realized I didn't have any experience working with children. At the time, I was going to school for art education and working as a server to pay for college. I began looking for jobs that would give me experience working with children. I started working as a nanny and soon found a job teaching Spanish to young children and their parents. I recall being nervous on my first day, but when the class was over, I could hardly recognize the person who had just taught the class. It was as if "somebody" had taken over my body and taught the class for me. It was amazing!

That very same day, I sat in an art history class and realized I was on the wrong career path. I literally walked out of the class, went to my advisor's office and changed my major to child development. After year of teaching Spanish classes to young children and their parents, I was asked to become the director of a new Spanish-immersion preschool.

With only a few child development classes under my belt, I was eager to take on this new challenge, but it required a break from college. I was amazed that I was tackling such a position without a degree, I felt smart and powerful. The first six months were a learning experience. I found myself to be a very effective Spanish teacher, but something in my gut suggested my teaching methods were wrong.

After the first semester, I realized that to be the best teacher and director she could be, I needed to go back to school so I could articulate what that unsettling feeling in my stomach was all about. Soon after leaving, I received a call from a parent of a previous student who wanted private lessons for his son. Ryan came from an English-speaking family who wanted him to be bilingual. Ryan became my best teacher, ranking right alongside my mom.

The first semester with Ryan was tough. As he was receiving private lessons, I felt they had to be very structured and theme-based. All lessons, activities, art activities, songs were focused around a specific theme. I created several different assessments and even encouraged him to start reading in Spanish way before he was even ready.

Ryan was very excited the first week I came to his house, but it only took about three weeks for him to start *hating* me being there. This was devastating to me because children in general loved playing and hanging out with me. I couldn't understand why he didn't enjoy my Spanish class. Surely it had nothing to do with the fact that they had a very strict schedule, a specific theme, and I was trying to get him to read in Spanish before he was ready. Sarcasm.

Luckily for all of us, at the start of the fall semester as Ryan was getting ready to start kindergarten, his dad asked me to keep the lessons more playful, since he was going to be in kindergarten all day long. This was the best thing ever. We basically just began playing in Spanish. The fact that I felt like I had permission to play in Spanish, rather than doing a tutoring lesson, created the freedom to build a real meaningful relationship.

I also was taking Dr. Atkins' play class in my child development program that semester, and it provided the reassurance I needed that the work with Ryan was the right way to go.

Lightbulb

I was so convinced that second-language acquisition and play went hand-in-hand that I made my journey with Ryan a major project for this play class. I interviewed Ryan on video and in Spanish about the different ways in which he had learned Spanish from me, and his favorite part about each different approach. And at the end of the interview, I asked him: "So tell me, out of all those different ways of learning Spanish, what do you think is the best way of teaching a second language?" I was convinced his answer was going to be "by playing".

Surprise! His first answer was: "with my dad." I completely ignored his answer and continued asking: "Okay, so what else?" Until he finally said: "by playing." This was not intentional, but I literally had convinced myself that play was the right answer. It wasn't until about two months later that I reviewed the video and realized that his dad really was the key factor in his language acquisition.

This was an "aha" moment and a great discovery in my teaching journey. Just as my mom had been the key factor in my language acquisition, Ryan's dad was the key to his learning. On that day, the concept of bilingual family was born. Now, Bilingual Family is my own Spanish-immersion program, where I help families become bilingual. Ryan grew tremendously with the program and is now able to speak, read, and write in Spanish. He even has mentioned the possibility of "ruling" the school one day.

With Ryan, the spirit of the teacher was guided by relationships. Think back to a person that impacted your view of the world. Maybe it was a mentor, teacher, relative, parent or friend. Chances are this influential person made you feel capable, confident, and helped you build your desire to learn. The premise of this book is that we learn through relationships and real meaningful interactions.

The method that we use at Bilingual Family and that we encourage families to use at home is the exact method that we will outline in this book. I hope that my journey as a learner and as a teacher will allow you to see the power that you have in your child's language-acquisition journey. It is important for you to understand that it will be a journey with ups and downs, but we promise the rewards are worth it. If you read this book and apply this method, then you too can become a bilingual family.

Second Language Acquisition is All About RELATIONSHIPS

THROUGH RELATIONSHIPS, WE learn about the world. We can all remember a time we learned something from a parent or another significant person in our lives. If we ask someone who their favorite teacher was, they smile and respond with a delightful description. People learn best when they are in a comfortable setting with responsive communications. Responsive communication extends, deepens, and strengthens language abilities. This is why the main theme of this book is how important relationships are in our quest to develop a second language.

One of the main reasons we ever want to genuinely have a conversation with someone is because we have a relationship with them, or we want to create one. Think about it. A baby's first words for the most part are "ma-ma" or "da-da," and why is that? They have a relationship with their mom and dad. Relationships are the foundation for language learning.

Process vs. Product

When you consider second-language learning, what are some of the emotions and feelings you get? Most of us think of a cold classroom with a heavy textbook, a long list of vocabulary words, verb conjugations, and a teacher/professor who is obsessed with correct pronunciation. Many times we are more concerned about getting an "A" grade on the test, so we memorize the vocabulary or rules without a need to use them.

My second language is English and I acquired it through real and meaningful interactions, but my third language, French, was not acquired in the same way. In fact, although I took four years of French in high school and two years in college, I can hardly call myself a French speaker.

How is this possible? It should actually be easier for me to learn a third language, especially with French being a romance language that shares so many cognates and similar sentence structures with English and Spanish. The answer lies in the approach to teaching, as well as in my intrinsic desire to learn the language. The approach was the same as any other language class you have most likely experienced – grammar-based, vocabulary-driven, and boring! My intrinsic desire was simply to be smarter, motivated by how cool it be to say that I spoke three languages.

Looking back, I realize that "being smart" was not a strong enough reason to learn the language. I had no burning desire to visit France, nor did I have any French friends I wanted to communicate with. It's not surprising to me that, even after taking five years of French, I can hardly consider myself an intermediate speaker. I do remember many helpful phrases, colors, numbers, family members, days of the week, months of the year, etc., but when I watch a French film or listen to a French song I have no idea what is being said.

The biggest difference in the methods I experienced in learning English and French is RELATIONSHIPS. When I was acquiring English, I had a desire to communicate with my mom and later with my friends. When I was learning French, I just wanted to look smart and get an A.

Here are a couple examples to illustrate the importance of relationships in second language acquisition.

Cousins

It was the first day after winter break, and it usually takes children a couple of days to get used to the Spanish language again after a break. However, today was different. Justin walked in speaking in Spanish completely. He was even saying words he had never said before and I was completely amazed. I told him, "Justin, what happened? Did you drink a magic potion?" Everything I was saying was in Spanish by the way, and the reason I said magic potion was because most of the children in the after-school program had been making magic potions before the break. It was a way to connect what I was saying to him, but he just laughed and continued speaking in Spanish, and this went on throughout the whole day. He was only speaking in Spanish.

Now, it's important to mention that Justin comes from an English-speaking family and both of his parents only speak English. They are very interested in learning the second language, but they are not native speakers or fluent Spanish speakers.

When his mom came to pick up Justin, I asked the same thing: "Did you give Justin a magic potion?" She laughed and then told me that Justin's cousins had been visiting during the break, and they are also English speakers who attend a Spanish-immersion school in Oregon. Because their cousins were speaking Spanish, it became a cool and fun thing for Justin and his brother, Charlie, to do. They really enjoyed speaking in Spanish with each other and seeing that their parents couldn't understand them. So because the cousins spoke Spanish, it became something real and meaningful to Justin and Charlie. This is just a quick example of how relationships really matter in second-language acquisition.

Little brother starts speaking

When I first met Nathaniel, he hated Spanish. His mom said he would literally cry if she played a movie in Spanish. After about a year in our after-school program, Nathaniel could understand almost everything I said in Spanish, but was still replying in English. Nathaniel's dad is a native speaker from Mexico, and his mom knows enough Spanish to get by and really tries her best to use it at home. But they were getting the same response we were getting at school. He was understanding everything at home, but only replying in English. Well, this changed practically overnight, and it all changed when his little brother started speaking.

His little brother, Matthew, had been attending our Mommy & Me classes once a week. And because he was exposed to the Spanish language before he started speaking at all – in English or in Spanish – most of his first words were Spanish words. When Nathaniel's little brother started speaking, mostly in Spanish, Nathaniel naturally wanted to play and communicate with him. He had no other option than to start producing in Spanish.

A New Environment

That's the social part of the relationships, but we also have relationships involving ideas, concepts and our environment, and not just with people. Lily showed us exactly that. Lily's mom and dad are native speakers, unlike the other two examples. They have been speaking Spanish to Lily for her whole life. She had been going to a child development center that was an English-speaking facility. All the children were speaking to her in English and all her friends, all her fun, involved English. When she came to Bilingual Family, I could tell she understood everything I was saying, but she wasn't producing in Spanish. But it only took about a week in our program for her to start producing. The silent period was very, very short because she had a relationship with the environment. She was now connecting Spanish to our playful environment. She saw

Spanish as "fun with friends and teachers." It's all about relationships – with a person, idea, or our environment.

Justin, Nathaniel and Lily illustrate two important principles in learning a second language. The first is the intrinsic need to use the language. For children, there is a deep intrinsic need to connect with others, and this is usually through their play, which is a non-threatening way of learning. If your child can play in the language that you want them to learn, then you can help develop that intrinsic need to use the language. Justin, Nathaniel and Lily show how children need to communicate to connect with others.

The second concept is that learning a second language occurs in the communication with someone who is meaningful to you. Nathaniel and Justin illustrate the importance of relational connections with a brother and a cousin. Such language connections can occur with family members, friends, and acquaintances. Even if you don't speak a second language, your child will learn better and create deeper connections to the language with you by their side because learning best occurs in relationships.

Now can you see why relationships are so important in second-language learning? So how do you build those relationships?

You have to understand the child. You have to understand their interests, skills and, most importantly, their development. In the next chapter we will share the two most important aspects of understanding your child – Child development, and guidance techniques.

UNDERSTANDING YOUR CHILD

U NDERSTANDING YOUR CHILD'S development is most important when trying to teach them anything new. When we have an infant and we notice they are getting ready to walk, we prepare the environment to support their new skill.

It is so important to understand your child's development, so you can be effective in guiding and nurturing them in all aspects of their growth. By understanding your child, you will be able to guide their capabilities. As your child grows physically, socially and intellectually, we adjust parenting to meet their needs. You must understand what is developmentally appropriate for your child so that you know when to make adjustments and when to challenge your child.

Many times, children are capable of learning much more than we give them credit for. At times, we expect too much out of our children and we create frustration. It is important to find the right balance so your child will love learning. The same is true when learning a second language. You must understand what your child is ready for and the best way to introduce a new language.

Here is a developmental chart with some examples of child development and how you can participate in your child's journey.

Infant Development		
	The Developing Baby	**Your Role**
Physical	The first 12 months bring many changes in growth of fine (reaching and grasp) and large motor movement, such as crawling, scooting, walking.	Provide plenty of tummy time; put toys out to develop reach. Use push toys to encourage movement such as pushing & pulling and walking. Plan time for play inside and outdoors.
Social/Emotional	Your infant develops security and attachments are formed. Feelings, emotions, and expressions will start to be displayed.	Gaze into your baby's eyes, sing, talk and read to your baby. Cuddle, rock, massage, and hold your baby. You cannot spoil an infant. Read and follow your baby's cues.
Thinking	Your infant starts category development, first use of language and gestures to communicate, develop concepts and meaning of words and items for the world they live in.	Play games, such as peek a boo, or this little piggy. Imitate baby sounds back and forth. Provide lots of experiences – field trips, parks and gardens. Read to your baby using different voices. Do not expose them to technology.
Language	Your infant starts the use of gestures and begins first speech with first words. Imitate familiar sounds.	Use lots of language, use parent-ease voice, read to your baby, use gestures and sign language, start using 2nd language during routines.

Toddler Development		
	The Developing Toddler	Your Role
Physical	Your toddler may be able to run and climb stairs, feed/dress themselves and manipulate toys. Toddler starts to explore everything around them.	Provide toddler with lots of moving activities such as climbing, running and dancing. Give toddler different foods to self-feed and opportunities to explore toys and safe household objects.
Social/Emotional	Your toddler may start to be interested in other children, may show negative or defiant behavior, and show an array of emotional expressions.	Be patient with the new ability to show emotions, use calming techniques to settle frustrations. Redirect (get attention onto something new) when negative behaviors arise, establish routines because toddlers need predictability.
Thinking	Your toddler starts to follow simple instructions, conducts mini experiments, starts to engage in make believe play and solves problems (sorting, shapes).	Provide toddlers opportunities to play with objects they can fill, dump and sort. Provide items and toys for them to categorize. Read lots of books to your toddler. Provide experiences where they can play with or beside other children.
Language	Your toddler starts with single words and then sentences. Uses words to get needs and wants. Language may not be fully understandable.	Use lots of descriptive words, sing songs together, give simple instructions Continue to use 2nd language in routines and story reading.

Preschool Age Development	
The Developing Pre-schooler	**Your Role**
Physical Your preschooler can kick, throw and catch a ball, climb and run, manipulates clay, draws and cuts with scissors. During this stage, children can be very active.	Provide opportunities for a preschooler to use their body and practice motor skills, such as park visits and lots of nature play. Provide experiences for child to use different media to create art and build.
Social Emotional Friendships develop, your preschooler may not always get along or agree with playmates but develops solutions to conflicts. May develop fears, is more independent, may have tantrums.	Provide play experiences with other children, assign chores or small jobs around the house to develop responsibility and independence. Discuss conflict solutions and how to be kind. Provide choices to avoid power struggles.
Thinking Your preschooler may tell stories, remember details, play simple games and develop strategies, solve problems and develop abstract ideas.	Use language that describes time and concepts such as bigger, have children retell stories, provide exposure to new things (museums, musicals, cultural events). Provide opportunities for child to engage in pretend play. Ask questions to get children to think.
Language Your preschooler's language should be understandable most of the time. Your child may engage in conversations, tell stories, ask lots of questions, sing, begin to rhyme words, ask for meaning of unfamiliar words.	Engage in conversations with children, talk with your child not at them, expose children to play opportunities with other children, relatives or people that speak 2nd language, engage children in using 2nd language through play and their interests.

31

School Age Development		
	The Developing Child	**Your Role**
Physical	Your child can engage in sports, dance, ride bikes and do other physical activities. Child develops and refines writing skills. Can create art and 3-dimensional objects.	Engage child in physical activities, encourage outdoor play, limit television time, provide materials to build and manipulate and items where they can be creative.
Social/Emotional	Your child cooperates, shares and friends become very important, likes to engage in family activities and plays games with others. Your child can display strong emotions. Compare himself/herself to others.	Provide opportunities for child to be social and practice skills. Model appropriate behavior. Use positive guidance techniques for behavior issues. Be flexible and offer choices and come up with options together.
Thinking	Your child understands concepts, is able to follow rules and stay on tasks. Develops preferences and his/her own ways of learning. Develops own interests.	Allow child to complete task without assistance. Support their interest. Assist in areas of learning that may be a challenge. Introduce new information in a variety of ways.
Language	Your child speaks clearly. Engages in conversations and expresses frustrations. Plays with language in songs, jokes and develops a wide arrange of vocabulary, greater memory and attention span.	Use high-quality language interactions with children. Expose to a wide range of vocabulary and experiences. Develop 2nd language acquisition together to promote usage, knowledge and relationships.

Aspects of your child's temperament, personality and even body language all are important to take into consideration when helping your child learn. For example, some children adjust to new environments with great ease, while others see change or something new as stressful. As a parent, you would have to consider how to adjust the situation for your child to make a successful transition.

Your child's personality is an important factor. A shy child may not verbalize with others for some time. Verbalization comes when children are comfortable and have a purpose to communicate. It is important to be patient and consider these aspects of development. By reading your child's body language, you know when they are too tired, playful, or engaged in learning. Use these cues to adjust your parenting. This will help you succeed in all areas, especially language learning.

Learning is a Natural Process

There are many strategies to encourage learning. I had the opportunity to study with a well-known education researcher, Constance Kamii. She once explained that learning happens when you have to make a decision about something. For example, your children have probably gone to the grocery market with you many times, but if you were ask how to get there, they probably could not tell you. Once they start to drive or take transportation, they have to think about the way to get there. They have to make decisions about where to turn, how far to go, and so they learn the directions.

When we learn math, we have to make decisions about which functions to use. For example, when a toddler first learns a word for dog, they call almost every four-legged animal a dog. When they realize other animals are not dogs, they have to make decisions about what to call the other animals. They may even go into a silent period (similar to language acquisition stages) until they develop a new category of animal names. When we have to make a decision about something, we learn. By allowing opportunities for children to make decisions, we are putting them into a learning state of mind. This could be done by simply asking questions with simple responses such as:

- It's cold outside, what do you think we will need to wear today?

- Help me decide some meals for the week?

- What would we need to buy at the store?

- What do you think about (current event)?

Questioning techniques can be good strategies for encouraging children **to think and communicate**.

Questioning Techniques

We can create learning opportunities by using questioning techniques. Asking children open-ended questions such as, why do you think that happened?, or what would happen if..., creates a situation where children to have to think. According to Bardige[1], we spend a lot of time talking at children instead of with children. To get children to think, we have to purposefully use questions. This strategy is also used in second-language acquisition. Many people recall that they learned a language when they were immersed or lived abroad for a period

---

1   Bardige, B. (2005). At a loss for words: How America is failing our children and what we   can do about it. Philadelphia, PA: Temple University Press.

of time. One of the reasons for this is that they had to make decisions about the statements, questions, and phrases they needed to use.

As in the above example with the toddler saying the word, dog, when we learn something we make categories in our minds, and we create relationships with the world. We only learn something new when we can attach the new knowledge to what we already know. We have categories in our minds for animals, social phrases, food etc. Decision-making leads to the development of more categories and vocabulary. The same process is true for language development. When we have to make a decision about what word or phrase to use, we learn. This is one reason why repetition is crucial in the learning process.

Modeling and Repetition

Children learn through repetition. For example, children love to hear the same bedtime story over and over again. Children like to do the same puzzle over and over. Repetition leads to mastery. When children learn to self-feed during their meal-time routine, they do it over and over again until they can feed themselves. They needed repetition, modeling, and lots of opportunity for this development to occur. Children need many opportunities to repeat actions.

Children naturally choose more challenge once they experience success. Creating a learning environment and atmosphere for this type of development requires effort, which can be fun and rewarding. One place to start is by providing children with age-appropriate materials, especially those that allow children to create and construct, which provides for a higher level of thinking.

You will need to use strategies to model, create opportunities for your child to think, and be prepared to repeat learning situations over and over again.

Creating a Natural Learning Environment

- Look at an environment from a child's point of view.
- Create safe, explorative surroundings.
- Make materials accessible.
- Provide materials that allow children to create and construct (art materials, blocks, Legos, household items, pretend objects, recyclable items).
- Provide time and space.
- Utilize outdoor environments and nature.
- Model and engage with the materials

Providing children with an engaging environment and many choices gives them the opportunity to think and respond, and cuts down on power struggles and unwanted behavior.

Guidance Techniques

One of the most powerful ways to build relationships and help your children learn and develop is to guide them. How you guide your child in infancy is very different from how you guide a school-age child. This is where knowledge of child development will help you foster and guide your child. The following are three key tools in building a relationship and guiding **your child**:

- Respect

- Focusing on what you want to see

- Choices

Respect

How do you teach respect? The best way to teach anything to your child is through modeling. So how can you show respect to your child? Well, you have already taken the first step, and that is to understand your child. When you understand your child's development and you understand your role in their development, you are showing your child respect. You will be able to create an environment that is respectful to your child, a "yes" environment, meaning an environment where they are free to choose and interact with the rest of the community.

A quick example of this would be if you have a 2-year-old and you don't want them to grab everything that could break around your house. You would put those things away, perhaps at a higher level where they cannot get to them. At the same time, you know they are exploring with all of their senses. They're going to touch everything and they're going to want to pick up everything, look at it, and open it. You want to leave things out which they can explore safely. You are respecting their development and their desire to learn through exploration.

If your toddler is in love with climbing, resist constantly saying, "No, no no, don't climb on the bookshelf, don't climb on the table, don't climb, don't, don't, don't." Instead, you can provide a space for them to climb. Perhaps take the pillows off the couch to set up a climbing structure and let them know that this is where they can climb. Because you understand their development and the stages of it, you will be able to aid them in growing and moving into the next stage of development in each domain (Physical, Cognitive, Language, Social/Emotional).

As you may have already noticed, the biggest theme in this book is that second language acquisition is all about relationships and the best way to build a relationship with your child is to develop mutual respect. We feel respected when our opinions are valued, our feelings are acknowledged, and we feel heard.

Active listening

The following is an example from our preschool classroom. It illustrates how problems can be solved and collaboration can be achieved when children feel heard and feel that their opinions are valued and respected. Jaden, 5, loved sitting next to his little sister, Sofia, 3, during snack time. At the beginning of the year, he was able to do this with no problems. However, as his sister started making friends, and other children started noticing how important it was for him to sit next to his sister – and what a big deal it was – they started wanting to sit next to her. Eventually, Sofia did not want to sit next to Jaden. While this started to become an issue, somehow Jaden always ended up sitting next to his sister and the issue was "resolved."

One particular day, however, Sofia decided that she really did not want to sit next to Jaden and wanted to sit instead between her two best friends. She gave a hug to Jaden and told him that she loved him, but that she was going to sit next to her friends. Jaden could not handle this response. He simply did not want to sit anywhere, not at another table, with another friend, except with his sister. He started hitting things and disrupting the class. At this time, I gave Jaden the option of sitting at a different spot, or coming with me to figure out a solution. He chose to come with me and we sat in the hallway trying to figure out what we could do to solve this problem. I gave him lots of ideas, but he was simply not able to cope with the problem at this time. We spent over an hour trying to figure it out, and in the meantime, snack was over and now he was even more upset because now there really was no way he could sit with his sister.

After the day was over, I reflected on this and decided to use a strategy from the book The Explosive Child[2], While Jaden was not explosive, I knew he didn't know how to control his emotions and how to problem-solve. The strategy I used was "collaborative and proactive solutions," from this book. It's basically really listening to the child. The next day, I talked to him when he wasn't upset, when he wasn't thinking about sitting next to his sister, and I simply said, "I noticed that you really want to sit next to your sister. What's up?" This is the exact language Green (2011) recommends. You state the problem, "I've noticed (blank). What's up?" It's that simple. Then you listen.

Jaden told me that he just loved his family and he wanted to sit next to his family. In that moment, I stated my adult concern

---

2   Greene, R.W. (2011). The Explosive Child: A New Approach for Understanding and Parenting Easily Frustrated, Chronically Inflexible Children. New York: Harper Collins.

or perspective. I said, "I understand. What happens is, when you refuse to sit and you start hitting things, it interrupts Ms. Silvia when she's reading a book. Remember that at Bilingual Family, we respect each other. Let's think about something that we can do when Sofia doesn't want to sit next to you. We can't really make her, but we can think of something to do."

He started thinking, and his first solution was simply to make her sit next to him. That's when I said that we couldn't make her do anything. He continued thinking and then he said, "I got it. How about we make a tag that says: I don't want to sit next to Sophie and we put it in my garage." I had to pause at this moment and really listen to him, because I went into this interaction already with my personal idea of what the solution could be. I had to really listen to him and ask him, "What do you mean by that?" He said, "Well if I put a tag (I think what he meant was a sign) in the garage that says: "I don't want to sit next to Sophie," then I can see it before I come to school and I can remember when I get here."

I said, "I understand. Well, maybe we can tweak it a little bit because you won't remember what you saw in the garage when you come to school during snack time. What if we make a tag or a sign and put it in the snack area? That way, when you come in, you can see it." He said, "Yep that sounds good." We got a piece of paper and I had him dictate what he wanted the paper to say. It said, "I don't want to sit by Sophie." Then I said, "Okay, if you don't want to sit by Sophie, where would you like to sit?" He said, "Sit next to Ms. Daniela." So we created two tags, or signs. One said, "I don't want to sit next to Sophie." The other one said, "I want to sit by Ms. Daniela."

Literally, 20 minutes after this interaction, resulting in this collaborative and proactive solution, we had snack time. Immediately, all the girls wanted to sit next to Sophie. I think probably because Jaden had made such a big deal about it, they were just intrigued to see what would happen if they sat next to her.

Jaden stood between the two snack tables and looked at the signs and "read them." Then he asked Ms. Silvia where I was going to sit. He sat next to the spot where I was going to sit. Problem solved!

All it took was spending time with the child, respecting their opinions, and really actively listening to their concerns and their solutions.

Developing Mutual Respect

- Active listening
- Quality time (plan it)
- Involve in rule making
- Speak in a calm tone
- Value ideas (try their solutions to problems)
- Teach and model manners
- Involve in planning family activities
- Ask their opinion

As mentioned throughout the book, RELATIONSHIPS are the foundation for second-language acquisition. Strong relationships are built and maintained with mutual respect.

Even when there is mutual respect, behaviors at times can remain a problem. One solution to developing a relationship with your child is to focus on the behaviors you want.

Focus

What behavior are you focusing on? Focus on what you want to see more of – you create your reality. That's why it's so important to put all your attention on what you want to see. When you say, "Don't yell, don't be silly, no running, no jumping on the bed, no, no, no..." You're focusing on what you do not want and, therefore, you're going to see more of it. When we say, "walk inside, or put your feet on the floor," we are telling children the behavior we want to see. We should always try to focus on the positive things. When you see that your child has produced a single word in Spanish, show them that you are excited and that it means a lot to you that they have put so much **effort** into learning the language. Because you have that relationship, they will want to have that exciting feedback.

The last tool is powerful. Using this technique can empower your child. When children feel they have some control of their lives, they are more willing to cooperate.

Choices

When we give children choices, we are giving them some control of their world. It is not giving in to our child; rather, it is giving them the opportunity to think and make decisions. Giving your child choices may make your life a bit less predictable, and may make your morning routines a bit longer. But giving your child the respect they deserve as members of our community will have positive lasting effects in your child's life, and potentially for the entire world. You are not raising a compliant follower; you are raising a leader, a problem-solver, a world-changer!

Imagine a day like this: You wake up and are told to go back to bed because it's too early. Later you are told to get up and make sure you don't forget to make your bed. You get dressed in the clothes which have been chosen for you. During breakfast, you are told to make sure you leave a "happy plate" even though oatmeal makes you anything but happy. Later, right as you start reading a book you've been dying to read, you are told to put the book away because you are going to the grocery store. How do you think you will feel by the end of a day like this?

Many children don't get to choose what they wear. They don't get to choose what they eat. They don't get to choose what time they get up. They don't get to choose anything throughout the day. If you allow your child to have lots of choices within their day, they'll be more likely to want to cooperate when it comes time to discipline or guide them, because they've had opportunities to be responsible and to take control of their own lives.

Guidelines for Choices

Only give a choice when there REALLY is a choice. For example, when it's bedtime, ask, "Would you like to wear the blue pajamas or the red pajamas?"

At times, let your child make choices which affect the whole family. Ex: Emma, you get to choose what we will have for dinner Friday night.

Now that you understand your child's development and how to guide them, you have the right ingredients to develop a deep relationship which, as we know, is the foundation for language learning.

How WE Learn Language

WHEN WE ARE born, we are primed to learn language. Language is our connection to the world and the key to our existence. We use language in our relationships and social interactions. We need language to be able to express our desires, needs, wants, and opinions.

Infants start to learn language with single sounds, babbles, first words, and then simple sentences. In learning a second language, the same process is used.

Before we explore the language-learning journey, it's important to debunk common myths about bilingualism.

MYTHS

Confusion

Often, parents worry that introducing two languages will confuse a child. They may even hear their children using both languages in one sentence. This brings in fear about confusion. The truth is that when children mix the languages – known as code switching – they are simply doing this because their brain picks up the first word that comes to mind. The child's goal is communication, and the child will use any means necessary to communicate. Naturally, they will pick whatever word comes to mind first, and use it in the sentence. As children get older, they begin to only code switch with people who are bilingual.

I was not aware of this until I started reading the research and realizing that I only code switch with my mom or other people who I know understand both languages. For instance, when I call my grandparents and I'm having conversations with them in Spanish, I never use any English words. This is not a conscious thing, it's subconscious. I know subconsciously that my grandparents only understand Spanish, so I only use Spanish words. With my professors in college or in the process of writing this book, I can't possibly use lots of Spanish words when I can't think of the English word, because I know that my audience or the person I'm speaking to only understands English. However, when I speak with my mom or anybody who I know is bilingual, like teachers of bilingual family, I often code switch. This is simply a sign of your brain's ability to adapt to people and situations.

Language Delay

Another concern parents have in raising bilingual children is the worry that introducing two languages might delay their language development. What often happens is that language development is measured by the number of words that a child is able to produce. For example, if a child knows and can say a hundred words, but their actual assessment is being done in English, maybe they only know fifty words in English. What is often viewed as language delay is simply a misunderstanding of language development, where only one language is taken into account, and we don't see that the child understands twice as much. They may not necessarily know the word for dog in both English and Spanish, but they may know dog in English and cat in Spanish. So they do know two words and perhaps the measuring method is only measuring one language, and therefore, cutting the amount of "known" words in half.

Children are Better Second Language Learners

I hear this all the time from parents, and adults in general. They believe children are better language learners than adults. Here's the reality. Given the right circumstances and given the right methods, adults could be just as effective as second language learners as children, and perhaps even better because they already have a foundation of language. Adults subconsciously understand language patterns and grammar structures in their native language. This understanding can serve as a foundation to build their second language. The issue is that the way that children are taught a second language is very different from the way in which adults are taught a second language. Children are taught through fun, play, songs, dance, and activities that are real and meaningful. Adults taking a language class, on the other hand, are often asked to memorize vocabulary, learn grammar structures, conjugate verbs, and so on. If adults would allow themselves to learn in the same way as children do, they would be able to access the "language learning powers" that children possess. The only advantage children have over adults is the ability to produce native accent.

Understanding the Journey

It's important for you to know the process for learning a second language. Most children really don't need an explanation of *how* the language is acquired, they just have fun and absorb the language naturally. But Justin, 8, didn't understand how you can learn a language without doing worksheets and repeating specific vocabulary. One day, he asked "did you even go to college? All we do is play".

I sat down and explained to him in English that this is how we learn a language – when we do things *in* the language. I used another student, who is advanced, as an example. I brought Ryan, 9, over and I asked him, "did we do worksheets? Did we sit down and repeat words? He said "no we didn't." For the next few weeks, I made sure to point out every time that Justin understood what I was saying. I said, "see, you understood everything I just said. That means you are learning the language." He would reply with, "Yeah, that is because you've used those words a thousand times." "Exactly, we learn language through repetition," I would reassure him. Justin needed that little explanation of how we learn the language so that he could say, "oh okay, I'm absorbing the information and eventually I will start producing." Justin not only understood the process of learning the language, but now is using a second language without fear.

In order to understand the process of acquiring a second language, we will review each of the Stages of Second Language Acquisition[3] and provide ideas on how to communicate with your child during each stage.

- **1st Stage** – The Silent Period (pre-production)
- **2nd Stage** – Early Production
- **3rd Stage** – Speech Emergence
- **4th Stage** – Intermediate Fluency
- **5th Stage** – Advanced Fluency

Stages of Second Language Acquisition

The Silent Period

Nature is wise. It allows a year to a year and a half for babies to simply absorb the language. Because of the baby's physiology, nobody expects them to talk when they're a week, two-months, or even six-months old. Babies have a year to year and a half

---

3   Krashen, S.D. & Terrell, T.D. (1983). The natural approach: Language acquisition in the classroom. London: Prentice Hall Europe.

of full immersion, 24/7, comprehensible input in their native language before they are expected to even say one or two words. Is this what happens in the language classroom? Absolutely not! In fact, students are expected to start repeating phrases and sentences on the first day, without getting the opportunity to first acquire the language and then produce. Understanding that the language must first be acquired before it can be produced is a key concept that must be understood in order for you to be successful in your journey to becoming a bilingual family. So if it takes a baby a year to a year and a half to start producing one to two words, how long should it take the child to start producing in a second language? I wish I had a simple answer, but it depends on the amount of input the child receives in the second language at home, in school and from the environment. If we wish to shorten the silent period, we must simply increase the amount of comprehensible input in the second language.

Ideas to Build Language

- Narrate everything you are doing (as much as possible).

- Make sure the communication is about real and meaningful things that are happening right NOW.

- Do not translate. Use any means to make yourself understood (gestures, props, drawings, associations with favorite movies, etc.).

- Do not force production.

* Additional resources in Ch. 7 for non-native speakers

Early Production

In this stage, the learner has had enough time to absorb the language and now has a bank account full of words that they can use and understand. It is important to note that these words come directly from the silent period. These words come from that zero-to-six months of absorbing the language. The words that you can expect during this early production stage are words your child has been absorbing during the silent period. Because you have built a strong relationship with your child and you have gone through this journey of learning a second language together, you are fully aware of the words he or she knows based on the words you have been using.

This is key because it will help you prompt your child in using those words as a response to questions, and it will help both of you feel successful in the language-learning journey. A few ways you can use to get one- to two-word responses are asking yes-and-no questions, or asking either-or-questions and we will cover this in more detail in chapter eight. Basically, asking any question to which the answer can be a one or two-word response. When you ask these questions, please make sure that they are real and meaningful.

In other words, do not use these one- to two-word responses as a way to test your child and to constantly be asking, "Is this blue or red?" or "Is this my nose or my ears?" That will take away the real and meaningful purpose of language. Instead of it becoming a conversation, your child will feel like he or she is being tested on a consistent basis. Remember, the sole purpose of language is connection and relationships, so make sure to keep yours strong throughout this journey.

Ideas to Encourage Early Production

Ask lots of questions:

- Either/or: giving possible responses within your question will increase the chance of your child replying in the target language.
- Yes/no
- Who
- What
- How many

Speech Emergence

This is a really fun stage, because in most cases there's a one-day turnaround where all these words seem to click and your child or you start producing full sentences in the second language. Again, it's important to note that the phrases that start being produced during this period come directly from all the input – all the language that has been absorbed – during the last two stages. In order to help your child produce sentences during this stage, ask "why" questions. Make sure the questions you ask have a response that requires words your child is familiar with. In other words, don't ask, "Why did World War II happen," if you've never talked about anything related to World War II. You can ask why questions about your daily routines or why questions about the game you're playing. Perhaps you've played this Lego game multiple times and they have enough vocabulary in their bank account to produce those responses.

During this stage, it's very possible that your child will make grammatical mistakes because the responses are a little bit more elaborate. It is crucial not to correct these mistakes. If you remember when you were a child, you made plenty of mistakes and it was only through listening to the correct way of saying these sentences, or the correct way of conjugating verbs, that you were able to eventually use the correct form. Here's a way to correct without correcting. If your child says, "I no like ice cream." Instead of saying, "No, it's don't, I don't like ice cream," you can say, "Oh, I know, I don't like ice cream either." You're basically giving them the correct way of saying it in your communication without correcting what it is they're saying. You're simply giving them the right way of saying it within your own phrases.

Ideas to Promote Production

Ask questions which require a simple sentence response.

- Why?
- How?
- Explain?

Intermediate Fluency

This is an exciting stage, especially for adults, because you're able to absorb things that are not only comprehensible but are also interesting. At this stage, there's less need for gestures, visual aids and context clues. The level of comprehension is much higher and the quality of the conversations is much deeper. A challenge that many of our parents face during this stage is the fact that their children's ability begins to surpass their own.

It is at this stage that parents may wish to have meaningful conversations with other native speakers, read books about things that interest them, and/or find a community of like-minded parents who want to raise bilingual children and have conversations that are at a more challenging level. While comprehension during this stage is excellent, it is important to note that you will still make grammatical mistakes. The best way to really understand the rules of grammar is to simply surround yourself with even more input, even more conversations in the second language.

Mastery of grammar is not achieved by memorizing rules and conjugating verbs, but rather by the constant use of the language and through real and meaningful interactions to which your brain can anchor those rules. The more real and meaningful interactions you have in the second language, the more the grammar structures will become second-nature to you.

Ideas to Increase Communication

- Tell stories of your childhood.
- Ask more in-depth questions:
- What would happen if?
- Why do you think?

Advanced Fluency

Congratulations, you're bilingual ... for now. As you may have noticed, we use the phrase language-learning journey often and there is a valuable reason for this. Being bilingual is not a final destination. It truly is a journey and, once you stop using the language, you will stop being bilingual. For this reason, it is crucial that you continue having real and meaningful relationships with people who speak the second language.

It is also important to note that, while you may be bilingual in many areas of your life, you may not be bilingual in all areas of your life. Here are a couple examples to illustrate this.

Losing Your Native Language

My father-in-law, Woo, was born and raised in Korea. He moved to the United States when he was eight and was encourage to mainly speak in English. His two younger brothers were born and raised in the United States and, therefore, only spoke English, and all his new friends were English speakers. He quickly started losing his Korean. The last person that he had a real and meaningful relationship with who only spoke Korean was his grandma. Once she passed away, he no longer had a need to speak Korean and he has now completely lost his Korean language.

Not Bilingual in All Subject Areas

While I am bilingual and have been told I have a native fluency in both English and Spanish, I went to college here in Oklahoma and all my vocabulary around child development and family life education came or was absorbed in English. I was very surprised when I went to talk to Miss Silvia, one of our teachers, about fine motor skills in Spanish and I was stuck because I couldn't think of the right terminology in Spanish. I was still able to communicate because I could say "small muscles". When she said "Oh, motricidad fina," it clicked. I knew the definition and had heard the term in the past, but was unable to use the correct term in that moment. This is a perfect example of why it is so important to have conversations about different topics so that you can expand the topics that you are bilingual in.

Ideas for Mastery

- Ask your child to retell stories or jokes.
- Take turns making up silly stories.
- Have your child teach you how to do something in the target language.

Stages of Second Language Acquisition					
Stage	**Preproduction**	**Early Production**	**Speech Emergence**	**Intermediate Fluency**	**Advanced Fluency**
Approximate Time Frame	**0-6 months**	**6mo. - 1.5 yrs** Total (6mo. - 2yrs)	**1-3 yrs.** Total (1.5 - 5yrs.)	**3-5 yrs** Total (4.5 - 10yrs.)	**5-7 yrs.** Total (9.5 - 17yrs.)
Comprehension	Has minimal comprehension	Has limited comprehension	Has good comprehension.	Has excellent comprehension.	Understands everyday conversation and normal classroom discussions without difficulty
Production	Does not verbalize.	Produces one- or two-word responses.	Can produce simple sentences. (prompted)	Can produce sentences without prompt.	Speech in everyday conversation and classroom discussions is fluent and effortless approximating that of a native speaker.
Vocabulary, Grammar, Pronunciation	Nods "Yes" and "No."	Uses key words and familiar phrases. Uses present-tense verbs	Uses key words and familiar phrases. Makes grammar and pronunciation errors.	Advanced vocabulary and sentence structure. Makes few grammatical errors.	Use of vocabulary and idioms approximates that of a native speaker.

We first learn words and then phrases to help us build our language repertoire. As we learn language, we are making categories in our brain that help us develop patterns and word knowledge, and to interpret word meanings. Patterns are in all languages. These patterns can include melodies, rhymes, and pauses used in language. By using patterns daily, even with simple phrases, one can start to develop a sense of patterns within a language. This is usually an "aha" moment. Once you identify a pattern; it gives you a sense of confidence in your own learning.

There are other strategies that help us learn language. We believe these are the most important ones:

- Repetition

- Understanding Messages

- Low Stress

Repetition

We learned our first language so easily because we heard the same vocabulary over and over and over as part of our daily lives. Our first words were words that we heard every single day, like mom, dad, bottle. The challenge with learning a second language is that repetition has to be real and meaningful. In other words, if you're asked to repeat "Good morning. How are you?" over and over again and you don't actually want to greet someone, and you don't genuinely care about how they're doing, repetition becomes boring and sterile.

We all know that repetition is key to learning a second language. The challenge is using repetition without being boring. This is especially important with young children because if you just repeat sentences that have nothing to do with their daily lives, it will become boring and they will not be interested in learning the second language. Many of us took language classes in high school and perhaps in college. In these classes, we were encouraged to memorize vocabulary lists and grammar rules, and to repeat commonly used phrases over and over and over. The results ... we still don't speak the second language, or third language in my case.

We do understand that repetition is important, so we're going to use it in a real and meaningful way. We are going to start repeating sentences during our child's daily routine. We're not simply repeating, "My name is Daniela" a hundred times so that I can memorize it. We are repeating sentences that are based on things that are happening right now, which are real to our children and to ourselves so that we can create connections with everything – the physical, the smells, everything that's happening – and those words. For example, the phrase "How many?" Can be used throughout the day and after you use this phrase often it will be part of your second-language repertoire. My challenge to you is to pick several sentences in the target language and use them consistently throughout your day. That's how you acquire the language through repetition of real and meaningful sentences and words. (See Chart in Chapter 7 & 8)

Understanding Messages

"We acquire a language when we understand messages"

- Stephen Krashen[4]

As we mentioned in the introduction, the way we learned our first language gives us a huge insight into the right way of teaching a second language. The way we speak to babies and the content that we use makes language comprehensible. We don't talk about abstract concepts or about concepts the baby is not yet familiar with. The majority of our conversations with babies are about *now*! What is happening right now, what is the baby touching, what is the baby eating, how does the baby's diaper smell right now. We do anything in our power to make what we are saying comprehensible. If we are talking about a stinky diaper, we may plug our nose or make a face. If we are talking about the baby's bottle, we make sure we have a bottle to show the baby.

We also narrate what the baby is doing. "I see you like your hands. Look at those little fingers. The baby is putting his hand in his mouth. how does it taste?" Although the baby does not know all the words you are saying, he or she understands the message and slowly begins to make connections to the words. Learning a second language is no different.

---

4   Krashen, S.D. (1981). Bilingual education and second language acquisition theory. In Schooling and language minority students: A theoretical framework. (p.51-79). California State Department of Education.

The following three strategies will help you provide comprehensible input to your child:

1- Talk about real meaningful things. This is where your relationship with your child will really empower you in introducing a second language. Because you have a strong relationship with your child, you know their likes and dislikes, you know their favorite color or their favorite animal and favorite foods, you know when they're happy and sad, and you know what lights them up. All this information you have about your child will help you talk about real and meaningful things in the second language. If you are not a native speaker or even a beginner in the second-language, don't worry! In chapter 7 and 8, we have provided routines and phrases to get you started.

2 - Narrate what the children are doing and what you are doing. If your child is choosing an activity, it's because it's real and meaningful to him. Take advantage of this and talk about what he is doing. If you have a limited proficiency in the second language, don't worry! Use what you know and what you're comfortable with. For example, if your child is playing with cars instead of saying "wow! It looks like your car is going really fast. Where is it going?" You could say "wow! fast car." You are still providing real and meaningful comprehensible input. Remember you are the most influential person in your child's life. Use what you can and don't be hard on yourself. Do not worry about mistakes. If you use a word in the incorrect context or form, you will eventually correct yourself and learn from it.

3 - Use any means possible to make yourself understood (except translating). This last strategy is probably my favorite, mainly because it allows you to be silly and supplement your communication in a creative way. This supplementation may include gestures, drawings, a change in voice intonation and volume, and even name-dropping of famous cartoon characters. Example: At Bilingual Family, every time we talk about something B I G, we use deep voices and usually open up our arms in a big circle. When we talk about something small, we use a high-pitched voice, squint our eyes, and put our thumb and finger almost touching. When you translate, your child's brain learns that it doesn't have to make sense of the content. Think about it. If you are always giving your child the answer, they don't have to make connections in their mind. Keep immersing them in the language and their brain will develop neutral bilingual connections.

Here's a quick video to help you further understand this concept

bilingualfamily.us/understandingmessages

Low Stress

If you ever took a language class in high school or college, I'm sure you can remember the dreaded presentation time. Or the class where the teacher randomly calls on students and expects them to reply with correct grammar and pronunciation. From my personal experience, I remember completely ignoring what the professor was saying because I was too busy practicing possible answers in my head and worrying about when I was going to be called upon. Stress actually inhibits language learning. Stephen Krashen[5] calls it the affective filter. This is basically what's going through your head during an interaction in the second-language. If your affective filter is low, meaning there is low stress, you are more capable of acquiring the language because the input is so interesting and real to you that you almost forget it's in a foreign language. If, however, your affective filter is high, meaning the interaction is stressful, your brain will be focused on managing the stress and it will not allow you to acquire the language.

I have seen this high-stress interaction happening a lot, even outside of the classroom. I've seen it when native-speaking parents demand that their children reply in the second language. Forcing children to reply in the second language is simply a recipe for disaster. In fact, forcing children to do anything can be a recipe for disaster. Instead of forcing, influence and encourage them by celebrating each and every time they reply in the second-language. This concept takes us back to the importance of relationships. If you have a strong relationship with your child, they will want to communicate with you and impress you, that is when production will happen naturally.

There needs to be no stress. If you are stressed out or self-conscious about your pronunciation or grammar, language learning is blocked. Do babies stress out about "learning" the language? NO! The baby is not stressed out. He doesn't think "okay diaper, diaper, that means this thing that's on my bottom and I have to remember that because it might be on the quiz tomorrow". No, there's no stress associated with it.

---

5   Krashen, S.D. (1985). The input hypothesis: Issues and implications. New York, Longman.

Another example: When a child first learns to write or first spellings, they do not spell correctly. Children use sounds they know to create words. This form of spelling is temporary. If we keep telling them it is wrong or focus on misspellings, then they stop attempting to write. Book or correct spelling will develop. Encourage the journey and respect risk-taking.

A key point to keep in mind when applying these three strategies is to make it fun. In the next chapter, you will see why making it fun is mandatory!

MAKE IT FUN!

A KEY DISTINCTION to recognize is that, in order to learn a second language, our focus must be on learning *in* the language, rather than learning the language. Here's what I mean. When you're learning about art or learning about a science experiment in the second language, the second language is naturally absorbed. You are so focused on what it is that you're learning about that the second language is almost naturally absorbed. Instead of learning the words and learning the grammar structures, and learning key phrases, you are simply learning in the language.

When a baby comes into the world, we don't address their language learning in the form of a lesson. We focus on their development..."Okay, you're ready to walk. Let's learn how to hold your spoon. Let's learn how to crawl." They're learning skills and we're just attaching language to them. It's not about the language; it's about the skills and the development. We learn content in the language.

I'll give you a quick example of how this concept-based learning can happen. My mom absolutely loves to knit. She's constantly making beautiful scarves, beautiful hats, beautiful things. One day she told me that she saw this specific knit pattern and she wanted to learn how to do it, so she found a tutorial on YouTube, an hour-long tutorial. It was in French. Now, my mom would like to say that she speaks French, but she does not. She knows a few words. Of course, if you know the English language and you know the Spanish language, there are a lot of cognates with the French language. But, she does not speak French.

However, she watched a whole one-hour tutorial of knitting in French, learned how to do the pattern, and by the end of it she said, "I know how to say needle. I know how to say yarn. I know how to say ..." She learned all this vocabulary for the following reasons.

First, the content was real and meaningful to her. That is the number one key. Second, when she was absorbing the vocabulary, her brain was not focused on memorizing that vocabulary or on translating what that vocabulary meant word-for-word. It was mainly focused on the enjoyment of the activity. Because she already had so much vocabulary in her native language about knitting, her brain was easily able to translate and capture those words that were going to be important in her life.

This can apply to so many other things. The concept of learning in the language rather than learning the language can be the key to your success with your child. This is why it's so important for you to have a strong relationship with your child. Because when you do, you know their likes, their dislikes. You know their skills and you're able to adapt the activities to match their interests and simply do them in the second language.

What I am about to ask you to do may seem impossible, but it can hold the key to your success. In this moment, make the decision that you're not going to learn a second language, but rather that you are going to learn in the second language. Making this decision can make all the difference in achieving this goal of becoming a bilingual family. In fact, Tony Robbins, a well-known motivational speaker, says that your life can change with just one decision. To decide means to cut off, so you basically cut off the possibility of any of your previous beliefs.

Most of us grew up believing that learning a second language was hard work and that it had to be painful. In fact, we have been made to believe that most learning, in general, will be hard and painful. By the time we get to high school, we think learning is painful for the most part. We have to decide to change our perspective in order to make this possible.

Promise me right now that you are not going to learn a second language, but rather are going to learn *in* the language. What does that mean for you as an adult? It means learning to cook in a second language, or learning an instrument in a second language, or watching a documentary in a second language about something that interests you. Doing whatever it is that you love to do, learning about whatever it is that you want to learn, and doing all the activities that you love in the second language, instead of sitting down, getting some textbooks and memorizing vocabulary, and learning sentence structures. Simply do what you love to do in the second language.

The same goes for your child. If your child loves science, then do science experiments in Spanish or in the second language. That decision will be the biggest key to your success. Now that you've decided to learn in the second language, let's look at some strategies to have the best time in the second language.

Strategies for Making it Fun

For the strategies for making it fun, we have created an acronym, CPR. We decided to go with CPR because, in a way, we are bringing you back to life, back to play. We are helping you remember the playfulness and the excitement you had when you were a child.

Play is one of the best vehicles for second-language acquisition. It brings all the necessary components into one. It's comprehensible, it's real and meaningful, it has very low stress, there is a lot of repetition, and it's based on relationships. Usually, you don't play with somebody unless you have a relationship with them. There's a famous saying that goes like this ... "You don't stop playing because you get old. You get old because you stop playing." We want to bring you back to your youth. We hope that this CPR will bring you back and you will be able to connect with your child at a deeper level.

Be Compelling

C Make the interactions with your child so interesting that you and your child forget you're speaking in another language. This is the exact way in which we learned our first language. We baked cakes, we built towers, we played board games, and we simply used the language as a vehicle to achieve those things. Make sure that each and every interaction you have with your child is compelling, and that you're simply using the language as a vehicle to have fun, as a vehicle to make things, as a vehicle to learn concepts. If you are in the early stages of your second language development, you can find the words that relate to things your child absolutely loves. Use those words, learn them together and this will help you in your bilingual journey.

Be Playful

P The second strategy for making it fun is to **be silly**. This comes naturally to some of us, but silliness is the currency of childhood. If you can bring out that inner child, you will be able to connect at a much deeper level.

I consider myself a silly and funny person, but there are times when I needed a little extra boost, and that is when I bring out my alternate personality. His name is Woof-Woof. Woof-Woof is a puppet, and he was born or made in Colombia. My aunt made it for me; she made a set of puppets for my graduation from child development. I think part of the magic of Woof-Woof is the fact that he is not made in the U.S. and is not made professionally, per se. So he looks very different from any other puppet or stuffed animal the children have seen. That gives him a certain personality and character that children can't resist.

When I feel I'm getting too serious, or I'm simply too tired to be playful and be silly, I bring out Woof-Woof because he can always deliver. I encourage you to get a puppet or think of a way to bring out that alternate personality. Each of us has some kind of playful characteristic, whether it is humor, sporty, curiosity, or creative. Dig deep to be playful. It will impact learning for both of you.

Playing with The Language

There are many ways in which you can play with the language. You can find silly connections to the word in your native language, you can say things with a strong accent, and you can even make up silly words that combine your native language and the second language. Here's a word we made up at Bilingual Family, and it is supermencanta, S-U-P-E-R-M-E-N-C-A-N-T-A. This word was created many years ago by one of our after -schoolers. It was created out of a child's necessity to fully express themselves. Here's what happened.

We vote on materials at Bilingual Family. We put something from the classroom in a suitcase and the children get to vote on that material. Originally, there were only two voting options: I like it and I don't like it. Soon those options expanded and we added I love it, so-so, I don't like it at all. One day there was a piece of material that was so compelling and interesting to our students that he said, "I don't just love it. I super love it." Since "love it" is me encanta, he simply created the word supermencanta. This word has been used by all of our students ever since. We are even trying to get it into the dictionary, so I have a huge favor to ask you. If you come across something, a thing, an idea, a food – anything that you super love – use the word supermencanta. When someone asks you what it means, you can explain the story and tell them that our community is trying to put this word in the dictionary.

Use Stories from Your Childhood

As your child gets older, ages 6 through 12, they have a strong desire to connect with you through stories. This is probably your best opportunity to share with them meaningful stories from your childhood and use them as lessons and guidance that they can go to when they no longer want to hear your stories. I was aware of the power of stories and I knew that theoretically children ages 6 through 12 really benefited in the long run from their parents or caretakers sharing meaningful stories that could connect with their current experiences, but this did not become apparent until the day I was picking up Ryan from school. We were in the car and there was silence for perhaps a minute and he randomly said, "Tell me a story."

I said, "What do you mean?" He said, "Tell me a story. Something about Troy or Helen, Achilles, my dogs, or when you were a kid. Something funny." At that moment I realized that I had told him so many stories of my childhood. He actually craved hearing the funny stories and just being able to connect with me at a deeper level because he could hear what I was like when I was his age. I also knew that he loved animals, specifically dogs, and that's why he loved hearing all the trouble my dogs get into every day. Please, take advantage of those precious years when your children still want to hear your childhood stories. We have even come up with a game for times when we run out of stories to tell. One of us will come up with a theme, which can be food or pets or school or anything that will refresh our mind and help us think of stories around that theme.

If you are in the early stages of your language-learning journey and you don't have the vocabulary or fluency to be able to share your childhood stories in the target language, you can find your favorite movies or books from your childhood in the target language and share them with your child. Children delight in learning about your childhood experiences.

Be Responsive

R This strategy will help you with your relationship, not only with your child, but with every single person around you, and with every single interaction you have with people, and animals. When you are present, when you are in the moment, it's almost as if you have developed a sixth sense. You will be able to connect with your child at a much higher level, and they will be able to respond to you much better when you are really invested in what you're doing in that moment. You're not thinking about what's for dinner, you're not thinking about what your boss said during the meeting, you are completely invested in this silly game, in the tickling fight, in building the biggest Lego house. You are one hundred percent invested in that moment.

Children may not be able to tell you, "Hey, are you paying attention to me? Are you in the moment?" They're not able to articulate the fact that you are not being present, but they are keen detectors of presence. Here are a couple of ways to develop your ability to be present. The first is my absolute favorite. Meditate or spend some time in silence or prayer; just spend some time with yourself. I learned this technique through reading The Miracle Morning(201) by Hal Elrod[6], and I highly recommend this book for your personal life as a parent, for your business, for your career. It will truly transform your life, and in this sense, it will actually help you become more present and become a better parent.

Second, turn off your phone or put it in a different room so that when you are playing with your child, you are fully engaged, and they have your full attention. Some research[7] shows that children feel unimportant when parents are on their phones too often. Other research shows parents spending too much time on their phones negatively impacts their interactions with their children. Make sure that, during the time you spend playing with your child, they get the message that they matter and that there is nothing more important to you in that moment than interacting with them, and playing with them.

Whenever you feel like you're becoming boring or moody, use **CPR**. Be **C**ompelling, Be **P**layful and Be **R**esponsive!

Don't you wish there was a way to tie everything you have learned so far into an actionable plan? Well there is a way and the best part is that you are already doing it... Routines! That is the secret sauce. Simply adding the target language to your daily routines. In the next chapter we will show you

6   Elrod, Hal. (2012). The Miracle Morning: The Not-So-Obvious Secret Guaranteed to Transform Your Life (Before 8AM). Hal Elrod International.

7   Radesky, J. S., Kistin, C. J., Zuckerman, B., Nitzberg, K., Gross, J., Kaplan-Sanoff, M., & Silverstein, M. (2014). Patterns of mobile device use by caregivers and children during meals in fast food restaurants. Pediatrics, peds-2013.

how you can start learning the target language together in only minutes a day!

THE POWER OF ROUTINES
A.K.A. THE SECRET SAUCE

O NCE WE SAW that the biggest predictor of language success in our students was the parent's interest in learning the language, we knew that we had to do something to help the parents use Spanish at home. We have created routines, like bath time, bed time, meal time, in Spanish so that you can use those at home

Routines tie everything we have been discussing thus far into a perfect, actionable package. During routines, we are having conversations with the people we love and care for, and for the most part, during the daily routines, we repeat the same phrases over and over, but in a real and meaningful way. In other words, we are talking about things that are actually happening and we're talking with people we care about. If you choose just one routine and you decide to use the target language during that one routine, by the end of the month, using those phrases will become second nature to you, and you'll be able to add another routine. Imagine that. In one year, you will be using the target language during 12 of your interactions with your child.

As a parent in the modern, busy world, you may say that you don't have any routines, that your life is hectic and unorganized. However, consider all the times you interact with your child throughout the day. Think about the things that you say to them every single day and notice the patterns or repetition that are built into your day. These are your routines. Routines are the second-most powerful tool in learning a second language. Of course, you now know that relationships are the number one tool.

Why Routines Matter

In the early days of our school, I began to see that the times when children were producing the most Spanish were not necessarily the times when there was instruction. Rather, production came at the times that were repetitive, the times that we were doing activities that were the same every single day. For example, we were able to have full conversations and interactions in Spanish during our snack routine. Children knew all the vocabulary such as place mats, napkins, cups, water, crackers, fruit, vegetables, table, chairs, trash, finished, and they were able to ask questions and answer questions. They were able to answer questions in Spanish based on what they wanted to eat, how much they wanted to eat, etc. This simple observation made me realize that the reason they were producing in Spanish was simply because they heard the same vocabulary in context every single day. It was real and meaningful every single day.

The Challenge with Using Routines

Now that you see the power of routines, you may be tempted to start using Spanish during all your routines. If you're a native speaker, this may not be a problem. However, if you are learning the second language, trying to do too much at once will overwhelm you and you will soon see learning of a second language as such a huge, overwhelming task that you will give it up. For this reason, it's imperative that you start with small steps, small consistent steps. In order to ensure consistency, we must develop habits. We must make the use of the second language a daily habit.

Developing Habits

There's a lot of research on habit formation. Some experts say it takes twenty-one days, some thirty, some sixty-six, and some say it may take as long as ninety days. For the purpose of this book we encourage you to use each routine from chapter 7, for 30 days before it becomes a habit. Once it becomes a habit, add on a new routine. Whether it takes 21, 30 or 90 days, the most important key in developing habits comes from the book, The Power of Habit by Charles Duhigg[8].

The goal is to start with such a small task that, in your mind, it seems ridiculous not to do it. I've been wanting to make exercise a daily habit for years. I would typically make the decision that I was going to work out, go to the gym for three or four days in a row, and then I would stop, take a week off, come back, take a two-month break. Finally, I decided to cancel my gym membership. I'm sure this has never happened to you. Right?

This is how I made working out a habit. It all started with a decision, and you'll hear more about the importance of decisions in chapter 8. This was a big decision. I bought an elliptical. For those of you who know me, you know that I'm pretty frugal and spending a lot of money on a piece of equipment is a big decision for me.

My next step was deciding that I was only going to work out for 10 minutes a day. When I told my husband this, after spending hundreds of dollars on this piece of equipment and moving everything out of one of our rooms to make space for it, he was confused. He said, "10 minutes? That's it?"

I explained to him that if I could make this task so simple in my mind, if I could fool myself into believing that it was just 10 minutes, then I would be able to make it a habit. Today, I have developed the habit of working out every single day(15min).

---

8   Duhigg, Charles. (2012). The power of habit : why we do what we do in life and business   New York : Random House.

How can you implement this concept into your language learning? Don't worry, before you start freaking out, we have done most of the work for you. In the next chapter, you will find four routines for each age group that will help you use Spanish at home in a real and meaningful way during your daily routines. The most important thing is that they each only take two to five minutes to implement.

Because you know that it's only going to take two minutes of your time, your brain will be able to consider this and decide to do it every single day. Now that you understand how to create a habit and the power of routines for language learning, let's look at some routines you can use with your child starting today.

You're already waking up, you're already eating breakfast, you're already telling your children to go take a shower, you're getting dressed. It's not something that is an addition to what you're doing. It's just complementary to what you're doing. It's not threatening in terms of time because we're very busy. You're already doing it, so why not do it in Spanish?

ROUTINES TO GET YOU STARTED

THIS CHAPTER WILL provide actual routines that you can use during four different daily routines. It also includes three different age groups, bebés (babies 0-2 yrs.), niños y niñas (boys and girls 3-5 yrs.), chicos y chicas (kids 6+ yrs.). The reason why we have divided the routines into three different age groups is because the way in which you speak to babies is very different from the way that you would speak to your school-aged child.

We also included the same four routines for each of the age groups because we understand that you may have two or three children that fall into different age categories, and we wanted to make sure that you wouldn't have to learn three different routines. While the phrases may be a bit different from one age group to the other, you will only need to focus on speaking Spanish during that routine with all of your children. It's meant to simplify your life.

Soon you can develop your own routines. In Chapter 8, we have provided a chart with commonly used words and phrases. These will help you develop your own routines to fit your family life.

IMPORTANT: *While the routines, common phrases and vocabulary examples provided in this book are in Spanish, please know our method and strategies can apply to learning any language.*

How to Use the Routines?

You can photocopy the routines we have included or you can go to our website, bilingualfamily.us/routines, to download the PDFs for each of the routines. Next, you will want to tape or hang up those routines in the area of the house where those routines take place. For example, if you're doing mealtime, you'll want to put that routine PDF in your kitchen or in your dining room, so that you can see it and it can remind you to use Spanish during that routine.

How to Use the PDFs?

We encourage you to look over the vocabulary and the phrases before you actually use them with your child so you can become familiar with the sentences. This will make it easier for you to use them during the actual routine. Also, because you may not be comfortable with Spanish pronunciation, we have included QR codes which are simply a shortcut to a webpage. These QR codes are linked to the audio for each of the routines. You can use your phone to scan the QR code and listen to the audio. We also encourage you to do this before you actually try it with your child.

QR Reader

To get the QR code reader, simply go to your app store on your phone or look for "QR reader app." Most of them are free, just pick the first one with the best reviews. Download it, and when you open the app, you will see a square. You have to use your camera to put the QR code inside of that square. It will scan it, and send you straight to the page where our audio sits. Make sure that your volume is on so you can hear the audio.

Here's a quick video to help you further understand this concept

http://bilingualfamily.us/qrcodes

Making it Stick

Now, that you're familiar with the audio and you have placed the PDF near the room of the house where the routine will take place, the next and most important step is to have consistency and to use this routine every single day. Most of these routines will only take two to three minutes to execute. If you do this every single day for a month, by the end of the month, this vocabulary and the phrases will become second-nature to you, and you'll be ready to add another routine. Imagine that.

If you add a new routine in Spanish every single month, by the end of the year, you will be speaking Spanish with your child 12 times a day. The best part about it is that you will be speaking Spanish during real and meaningful interactions, so let's get started.

BEBÉS

We talk to infants much differently than we talk to other age groups. With infants, we use words to label everything. We use lots of gestures and pointing. We use descriptions and relate them to objects. We narrate their world by describing details such as what the baby is doing and what we are doing. We introduce them to new objects, concepts and people through messages they understand.

Hora de Levantarse
Time to wake up

¡Buenos días bebé! - Good morning baby!

Es hora de levantarse - It's time to wake up

Es hora de empezar tu día - It's time to start your day

Abre tus ojitos - Open your little eyes

¡Qué ojos_____tan lindos! - What beautiful ____eyes!

Cucú te veo - Peek-a-boo

Aquí está(n)_____ - Here is(are)_____

Vamos a cambiar tu pañal - Let's change your diaper

Vamos al baño - Let's go to the bathroom

Azules - Blue
Cafés - Brown
Verdes - Green

Tu cabeza - Your head
Tu nariz - Your nose
Tu boca - Your mouth

Tus manos - Your hands
Tus piernas - Your legs
Tus orejas - Your ears
Tus pies - Your feet

Vocabulary   Song

Buenos Días - Good Morning

Buenos días,	Good morning,
Buenos días	Good morning
¿Cómo estás?	How are you? How
¿Cómo estás?	are you?
Muy bien gracias,	Very well thank
Muy bien gracias	you, Very well
	thank you
¿Y tú? ¿Y tú?	And you? And you?

Libro - Book

Es La Hora De... (Spanish Edition) - by
Bruce McMillan

Hora de Vestirse
Time to get dressed

¡Es hora de vestirse! - It's time to get dressed!

Vamos a buscar en tu armario/clóset - Let's search in your dresser/closet

Necesitamos una camisa - We need a shirt

Aquí están las camisas - Here are the shirts

¿Quieres la amarilla o la verde? - Do you want the yellow one or the green one?

Un brazo por aquí...un brazo por acá - One arm over here...one arm over there

¡Estás vestido! - You're dressed!

La camiseta - T-Shirt	**Rojo(a)** - Red
La camisa - Shirt	**Verde** - Green
El pantalón - Pants	**Azul** - Blue
El pantalón corto - Shorts	**Gris** - Gray
	Blanco(a) - White
	Negro(a) - Black
El vestido - Dress	**Amarillo(a)** - Yellow
la falda - Skirt	**Morado(a)** - Purple
Los calcetines - Socks	**Anaranjado(a)** - Orange
Los zapatos - Shoes	**Café/Marrón** - Brown
El sombrero - Hat	

Vocabulary   Song

La Ropa - Clothing

Sombrero, camisa, pantalones y zapatos	Hat, shirt, pants and shoes
Sombrero, camisa, pantalones y zapatos	Hat, shirt, pants and shoes
Camiseta y los shorts	T-shirt and shorts
Camiseta y los shorts	T-shirt and shorts

Libro - Book

Azul el sombrero, verde el sombrero - by Sandra Boynton

Hora de Desayunar
Time to eat breakfast

¡Es hora de desayunar! - It's time for breakfast!

Vamos a tu silla - Let's go to the your chair

¿Cuál babero quieres? - Which bib do you want?

Un plato para ti, un plato para mí - A plate for you, a plate for me

¿Quieres tomar/comer leche o jugo? - Would you like to drink/eat milk or juice?

¡Qué rico! - Yummy!

¿Quieres más? - Do you want more?

¿Necesitas una servilleta? - Do you need a napkin?

¿Ya terminaste? - Are you done?

Plato - Plate
Vaso - Cup
Cuchara - Spoon
Servilleta - Napkin
Individual - Placemat

Cereal - Cereal
Huevos - Eggs
Yogur - Yogurt
Leche - Milk
Jugo - Juice

Fruta - Fruit
Manzana - Apple
Plátano - Banana

Durazno - Peach
Aguacate - Avocado
Arándanos - Blueberries

Vocabulary   Song

El pollito Po - The little chick Po

Estaba el pollito Po, sentado comiendo arroz El arroz estaba caliente y el piquito se quemó.	The chick Po was sitting eating rice. The rice was hot and his beak burned.
La culpa la tienes tú... La culpa la tengo yo... Por no darle cuchara, ni cuchillo ni tenedor.	It's your fault ... It's my fault ... For not giving it a spoon, or a knife or a fork.

Libro - Book

Hmm, qué rica mosca - by Paul Harrison

Hora de Dormir
Time to sleep

¡Es Hora de dormir! - It's bed time!

Cepíllate los dientes - Brush your teeth

Vamos a tu cuarto - Let's go to your room

¿Dónde está tu piyama? - Where are your pj's?

¿Quieres la amarilla o la verde? - Do you want the yellow ones or the green ones?

Vamos a leer un libro - Let's read a book

¿Cuál quieres leer? - Which one do you want to read?

Buenas noches luna/estrellas - Good night moon/stars

Buenas noches ____ - Good night ____

Un besito - A little kiss

Piyama - Pajamas	**Rojo(a)** - Red
Cobija - Blanket	**Anaranjado(a)** - Orange
Almohada - Pillow	**Azul** - Blue
Pantuflas - Slippers	**Café/Marrón** - Brown
Peluche - Stuffed animal	**Amarillo(a)** - Yellow
	Gris - Gray
	Verde - Green
	Negro(a) - Black
	Morado(a) - Purple
	Blanco(a) - White

Vocabulary   Song

Los pollitos - The little chickens

Los pollitos dicen	The little chicks says
pío, pío, pío,	peep, peep, peep,
cuando tienen hambre,	when they are hungry, when
cuando tienen frío.	they are cold.
La gallina busca el maíz y el	The hen looks for corn and
trigo,	wheat,
les da la comida y les presta	she gives them food, and
abrigo.	grants them shelter.
Bajo sus dos alas,	Under mama's wings,
acurrucaditos,	huddling up,
hasta el otro día, duermen	until the next day, sleep the
los pollitos.	little chicks.

Libro - Book

Buenas Noches Luna - by Margaret Wise

NIÑOS

With preschool age children, this age group is very inquisitive. They want explanations for everything. All the why questions may seem annoying, but are great ways to teach and converse with your child. Children at this age also learn from modeling. They pick up on how to be polite and social phrases to say, such as good morning. This is a time for parents to model appropriate language. Preschool children's brains are very active at this stage and they learn words rapidly. This is a time to expose children to lots of vocabulary. The best way to do this is through their environment and experiences. Remember vocabulary and social skills will have a lasting impact, so use this time to teach.

Hora de Levantarse
Time to wake up

¡Buenos días Eli! - Good morning Eli!

Es hora de levantarse - It's time to wake up

Hoy tienes Preescolar - Today you have Preschool

Hoy vamos a ▮▮ - Today we're going to ▮▮

¡Qué divertido! - How Fun!

Mira, son las ▮▮ **de la mañana** - Look, it's ▮▮ in the morning

Ya salió el sol - The sun is out

Hay nubes, y - There are clouds, and

Ve al baño, por favor - Go to the bathroom, please

Y cepíllate los dientes - And brush your teeth

5 Cinco - 5 Five	**Sol** - Sun
6 Seis - 6 Six	**Nubes** - Clouds
7 Siete - 7 Seven	**Lluvia** - Rain
8 Ocho - 8 Eight	**Nieve** - Snow
9 Nueve - 9 Nine	**Viento** - Wind

La case de _ - _'s house
El parque - The park
La tienda - The store

Vocabulary   Song

Buenos Días - Good Morning

Buenos días, **Buenos días**	Good morning, Good morning
¿Cómo estás? **¿Cómo estás?**	How are you? How are you?
Muy bien gracias, **Muy bien gracias**	Very well thank you, Very well thank you
¿Y tú? ¿Y tú?	And you? And you?

Libro - Book

Es La Hora De... (Spanish Edition) - by
Bruce McMillan

Hora de Vestirse
Time to get dressed

¡Es hora de vestirse! - It's time to get dressed!

Vamos a buscar en tu armario/clóset - Let's search in your dresser/closet

Necesitamos una camisa - We need a shirt

Aquí están las camisas - Here are the shirts

¿Quieres la amarilla o la verde? - Do you want the yellow one or the green one?

Un brazo por aquí...un brazo por acá - One arm over here...one arm over there

¿Dónde está tu pantalón? - Where are your pants?

¡Estás vestido! - You're dressed!

La camiseta - T-Shirt	**Rojo(a)** - Red
La camisa - Shirt	**Verde** - Green
El pantalón - Pants	**Azul** - Blue
El pantalón corto - Shorts	**Gris** - Gray
	Blanco(a) - White
El vestido - Dress	**Negro(a)** - Black
la falda - Skirt	**Amarillo(a)** - Yellow
Los calcetines - Socks	**Morado(a)** - Purple
Los zapatos - Shoes	**Anaranjado(a)** - Orange
El sombrero - Hat	**Café/Marrón** - Brown

Vocabulary   Song

La Ropa - Clothing

Sombrero, camisa, pantalones y zapatos	Hat, shirt, pants and shoes
Sombrero, camisa, pantalones y zapatos	Hat, shirt, pants and shoes
Camiseta y los shorts	T-shirt and shorts
Camiseta y los shorts	T-shirt and shorts

Libro - Book

Azul el sombrero, verde el sombrero -
by Sandra Boynton

Hora de Desayunar
Time to eat breakfast

¡Es hora de desayunar! - It's time for breakfast!
Vamos al la mesa - Let's go to table
Busca tu lugar - Find your spot
¿Cuál individual quieres? - Which placemat do you want?
Un plato para ti, un plato para mí - A plate for you, a plate for me
¿Quieres tomar/comer leche o jugo? - Would you like to drink/eat milk or juice?
¡Qué rico! - Yummy!
¿Quieres más? - Do you want more?
¿Necesitas una servilleta? - Do you need a napkin?
¿Ya terminaste? - Are you done?

Plato - Plate	Cereal - Cereal
Vaso - Cup	Fruta - Fruit
Cuchara - Spoon	Tostada - toast
Cuchillo - Knife	Huevos - Eggs
Tenedor - Fork	Leche - Milk
Servilleta - Napkin	Agua - Water
Individual - Placemat	Jugo - Juice

Vocabulary   Song

El pollito Po - The little chick Po

Estaba el pollito Po, sentado comiendo arroz El arroz estaba caliente y el piquito se quemó.	The chick Po was sitting eating rice. The rice was hot and his beak burned.
La culpa la tienes tú... La culpa la tengo yo... Por no darle cuchara, ni cuchillo ni tenedor.	It's your fault ... It's my fault ... For not giving it a spoon, or a knife or a fork.

Libro - Book

Hmm, qué rica mosca - by Paul Harrison

Hora de Dormir
Time to sleep

¡Es Hora de dormir! - It's bed time!

Cepíllate los dientes - Brush your teeth

Vamos a tu cuarto - Let's go to your room

¿Dónde está tu(s) piyama? - Where are your pj's?

¿Quieres la amarilla o la verde? - Do you want the yellow ones or the green ones?

Vamos a leer un libro - Let's read a book

¿Cuál quieres leer? - Which one do you want to read?

Buenas noches luna/estrellas - Good night moon/stars

Buenas noches _____ - Good night _____

Un besito - A little kiss

Piyama - Pajamas	**Rojo(a)** - Red
Cobija - Blanket	**Anaranjado(a)** - Orange
Almohada - Pillow	**Azul** - Blue
Pantuflas - Slippers	**Café/Marrón** - Brown
Peluche - Stuffed animal	**Amarillo(a)** - Yellow
	Gris - Gray
	Verde - Green
	Negro(a) - Black
	Morado(a) - Purple
	Blanco(a) - White

Vocabulary   Song

Los pollitos - The little chickens

Los pollitos dicen	The little chicks says
pío, pío, pío,	peep, peep, peep,
cuando tienen hambre,	when they are hungry, when
cuando tienen frío.	they are cold.
La gallina busca el maíz y el	The hen looks for corn and
trigo,	wheat,
les da la comida y les presta	she gives them food, and
abrigo.	grants them shelter.
Bajo sus dos alas,	Under mama's wings,
acurrucaditos,	huddling up,
hasta el otro día, duermen	until the next day, sleep the
los pollitos.	little chicks.

Libro - Book

Buenas Noches Luna - by Margaret Wise

CHICOS

School age children go through stages where they talk constantly or where you can hardly get them to talk to you at all. Since children at this age are quite capable of having conversations, it is important to engage them, especially about their own ideas and interests. Children at this age like to play with language and take risks. During this time, ask lots questions to get a responses, share jokes, and expose them to music, literature and rich discussions to expose them to language. Use this opportunity to expand your child's capability to learn a second language. They may even surpass you.

Hora de Levantarse
Time to wake up

¡Buenos días <u>Alex</u>! - Good morning <u>Alex</u>!

Es hora de levantarse - It's time to wake up

*5 minutos más, por favor - 5 more minutes, please

Son las ___ de la mañana - it's ___ in the morning

Hoy tienes escuela y después tienes ___ - Today you have school and after you have ___

¡Qué divertido! - How fun!

Después, vamos a ___ - After, we are going to ___

¡Listo, calisto! A levantarse - Ready, Fredy! Get up

Es hora de desayunar/vestirse - It's time to eat breakfast/get dressed

5 Cinco - 5 Five	Fútbol - Soccer
6 Seis - 6 Six	Fútbol Americano - Football
7 Siete - 7 Seven	Clase de baile - Dance class
8 Ocho - 8 Eight	Clase de música - Music class
9 Nueve - 9 Nine	

La case de _ - _'s house
El parque - The park
La tienda - The store

Vocabulary   Song

Buenos Días - Good Morning

Buenos días,	Good morning,
Buenos días	Good morning
¿Cómo estás?	How are you? How
¿Cómo estás?	are you?
Muy bien gracias,	Very well thank
Muy bien gracias	you, Very well
	thank you
¿Y tú? ¿Y tú?	And you? And you?

Libro - Book

Es La Hora De... (Spanish Edition) - by Bruce McMillan

Hora de Vestirse
Time to get dressed

¡Es hora de vestirse! - It's time to get dressed!

¿Qué quieres ponerte? - What do you want to wear?

*Quiero ponerme... - I want to wear...

*camisa verde - green shirt

*pantalón azul - blue pants

*y zapatos rojos - and red shoes

Vístete - Get dressed

No olvides tu sombrero - Don't forget your hat

¡Listo, calisto! - Ready, Fredy!

¡Estás vestido! - You're dressed!

La camiseta - T-Shirt	**Rojo(a)** - Red
La camisa - Shirt	**Verde** - Green
El pantalón - Pants	**Azul** - Blue
El pantalón corto - Shorts	**Gris** - Gray
	Blanco(a) - White
El vestido - Dress	**Negro(a)** - Black
la falda - Skirt	**Amarillo(a)** - Yellow
Los calcetines - Socks	**Morado(a)** - Purple
Los zapatos - Shoes	**Anaranjado(a)** - Orange
El sombrero - Hat	**Café/Marrón** - Brown

Vocabulary

Song

La Ropa - Clothing

Sombrero, camisa, pantalones y zapatos	Hat, shirt, pants and shoes
Sombrero, camisa, pantalones y zapatos	Hat, shirt, pants and shoes
Camiseta y los shorts	T-shirt and shorts
Camiseta y los shorts	T-shirt and shorts

Libro - Book

Azul el sombrero, verde el sombrero - by Sandra Boynton

Hora de Desayunar
Time to eat breakfast

¡Es hora de desayunar! - It's time for breakfast!

Vamos al comedor - Let's go to the dining room

¿Cuál individual quieres? - Which placemat do you want?

Ayudame a poner la mesa - Help me set the table

Un plato para ti, un plato para mí - A plate for you, a plate for me

¿Qué quieres tomar/comer? - What would you like to drink/eat?

*Quiero tomar/comer leche - I want to drink/eat milk

*¡Qué rico! - Yummy!

¿Quieres más? - Do you want more?

¿Necesitas una servilleta? - Do you need a napkin?

¿Ya terminaste? - Are you done?

*Ya terminé - I have finished

Plato - Plate	Cereal - Cereal
Vaso - Cup	Fruta - Fruit
Cuchara - Spoon	Tostada - toast
Cuchillo - Knife	Huevos - Eggs
Tenedor - Fork	Leche - Milk
Servilleta - Napkin	Agua - Water
Individual - Placemat	Jugo - Juice

Vocabulary   Song

El pollito Po - The little chick Po

Estaba el pollito Po, sentado comiendo arroz El arroz estaba caliente y el piquito se quemó.	The chick Po was sitting eating rice. The rice was hot and his beak burned.
La culpa la tienes tú... La culpa la tengo yo... Por no darle cuchara, ni cuchillo ni tenedor.	It's your fault ... It's my fault ... For not giving it a spoon, or a knife or a fork.

Libro - Book

Hmm, qué rica mosca - by Paul Harrison

Hora de Dormir
Time to sleep

¡Es Hora de dormir! - It's bed time!

Cepíllate los dientes - Brush your teeth

Vamos a tu cuarto - Let's go to your room

¿Dónde está tu(s) ▓▓ **?** - Where are your ▓▓ ?

¿Quieres la ▓▓ **o la** ▓▓ **?** - Do you want the

▓▓ ones or the ▓▓ ones?

Vamos a leer un libro - Let's read a book

¿Cuál quieres leer? - Which one do you want to read?

Buenas noches luna/estrellas - Good night moon/stars

Buenas noches ___ - Good night ___

Un besito - A little kiss

Mañana tienes ▓▓ - Tomorrow you have ▓▓

Piyama - Pajamas	**Rojo(a)** - Red
Cobija - Blanket	**Anaranjado(a)** - Orange
Almohada - Pillow	**Azul** - Blue
Pantuflas - Slippers	**Café/Marrón** - Brown
	Amarillo(a) - Yellow
Fútbol - Soccer	**Gris** - Gray
Fútbol Americano - Football	**Verde** - Green
Clase de baile - Dance class	**Negro(a)** - Black
Clase de música - Music class	**Morado(a)** - Purple
	Blanco(a) - White

Vocabulary   Song

Los pollitos - The little chickens

Los pollitos dicen	The little chicks says
pío, pío, pío,	peep, peep, peep,
cuando tienen hambre,	when they are hungry, when
cuando tienen frío.	they are cold.
La gallina busca el maíz y el trigo,	The hen looks for corn and wheat,
les da la comida y les presta abrigo.	she gives them food, and grants them shelter.
Bajo sus dos alas,	Under mama's wings,
acurrucaditos,	huddling up,
hasta el otro día, duermen los pollitos.	until the next day, sleep the little chicks.

Libro - Book

Buenas Noches Luna - by Margaret Wise

DREAM, DO, REVIEW – THE ROADMAP FOR YOUR JOURNEY

MANY OF US have been given the ill advice to separate work and life, work and home, to put our life into separate compartments. As I was struggling to create a title for this chapter, the words dream, do, and review came to mind. These were not random words because six months prior to writing this book, I did a TEDx Talk about entrepreneurship titled Dream, Do, Review. My entrepreneurship dream was creating Bilingual Family, and helping families raise bilingual children. I am so grateful to live out my dream every day.

While I struggled with the idea of mixing this entrepreneurship idea with language learning and helping families raise bilingual children, *I was struck by the application of this concept and how it can truly be applied to anything you want to bring into existence.* As I write this, I am emotionally inspired, which is one of the components of the "dream." This physical emotion tells me I'm on the right track. It tells me I chose the right title.

DREAM

Do you remember how to dream? How to really dream and create a whole reality in your mind? This is the first step in your journey. Close your eyes and imagine what it would feel like to become a bilingual family. To have meaningful full conversations with your child in the target language. To visit other countries and be able to interact with the community. Play this out in your mind, and feel it. Feel it as if you were actually there.

Now, I want you to reflect on what it felt like to be there, to have the dream accomplished. Were you moved? Did you cry? Did you feel something inside of you light up? If you answered yes to any of these questions, chances are you will become a bilingual family, because it matters to you, because the dream is bigger than yourself and it will have an impact on your family and the world.

Things to keep in mind while pursuing your dream:

Mindset

One of the biggest things that can make or break your ability to raise a bilingual child is your mindset. In her book Mindset, Carol Dweck[9] describes two kinds of mindsets: the fixed mindset and the growth mindset. The kind of mindset you need in order to learn a second language is the growth mindset. You need to understand that all of our abilities can be developed. Our intelligence, our creativity and our language skills are not stagnant. There is always room for growth. By reading this book, you already have taken a huge step toward improving your language-learning and teaching skills. Now that you've decided to go on this journey with a growth mindset, let's look at some practical tips to help you along the journey.

A Marathon Not a Sprint

Language-learning is a marathon, not a sprint. With our current fast-paced lifestyles, it's easy to get frustrated when we don't learn a language quickly, and it's easy to forget how long it actually takes to effectively learn a language. Many of the problems we face in the current teaching of second languages could be fixed if we actually considered the time it takes to learn a language.

---

9   Dweck, C. S. (2006). Mindset: The new psychology of success. New York: Random House.

Language-learning in the school system would not be a two-year event in high school. It would rather be a lifelong journey. Children would start learning the second language early on and ideally with the same teacher or teachers who knew the student's background, the student's likes, dislikes, and really tried their best to create a relationship with that student.

A relationship can't be made in a semester or a year or two years. This is why it's so crucial to use relationships as the best teacher of the second language. Students would not be required to take a test after each module or after each theme. Instruction would be based on real and meaningful interactions rather than memorization of vocabulary lists and verbs. Learning would happen in a stress-free and playful atmosphere and all learning would be dictated by the student's interests.

A language classroom like this one may sound like a utopia, but this is exactly what we are creating at Bilingual Family – a place where families can take the long journey together in learning a second language. Where relationships are the most important thing, where there's low stress, repetition through real and meaningful interactions, and most importantly where our teaching is guided by the student's interest. We've written this book because we know that, with the right tools, techniques and strategies, you too can create this language-learning utopia in your own home.

Now that you understand what this dream will entail, the steps it will take, and most importantly the mindset you must adopt to make your dream a reality. The next thing you must do is DO.

DO

Don't wait until you write out the perfect plan for using the target language, or what time of day you're going to do it. Don't wait for the Amazon delivery to come with all the books you need to start your journey. Don't go shopping to get language resources. Simply **DO**! Simply start.

As soon as you make the decision to become a bilingual family, as soon as you realize that it is the right kind of dream, start doing. If you only know the numbers, start using them; if you only know the colors, start using the colors.

If you don't know any Spanish, use some of the resources we have provided in this book to help you start using Spanish, and if you are a native speaker start using the target language with your child right now. Fluency comes through action, through speaking, not through thinking and planning. In this section we have provided strategies to help you get started even if you have a very limited knowledge of the language.

Baby Steps

> A journey of 1,000 miles begins with a single step.
>
> – Lao Tzu

The key to taking the first step in your language learning journey is understanding exactly where you are and not being afraid of using what you know to help your child learn a second language. For example, if you only know the numbers, every time you use the numbers in a conversation, use them in the target language. On page 122, you will see a chart, which will provide simple words and phrases that can be used to connect with all of the vocabulary you know in Spanish. You will be surprised to see how much Spanish you can use during your everyday routines by just using these *key* words and phrases to help you incorporate what you know in a practical, real and meaningful way.

Part of the beauty of learning a second language with your child is the fact that most of the conversations you will have will be simple, concrete, and feature very simple sentence structures. This is especially true with babies and very young children. Ideally, if you start this learning journey when your child is a baby, you can develop your vocabulary as your child grows and is able to understand more complex sentences and vocabulary. Decide what your first step will be and start today. You will be glad you did and your child will thank you for it.

Start Small

One of the biggest challenges our parents share with us is the fact that their children may be understanding everything in Spanish, but they're not actually producing. How can we help children start producing? A very simple way to do this is to give options within the question. For example, if you didn't know any English and I showed you a banana and I showed you an apple, and I asked, "Would you like a banana or would you like an apple?" You're able to hear those two words within the question, and you're able to produce, because you heard the words. You saw what I was talking about, and you were able to make that connection between the word and the object. Because you heard those words within the question, it is a lot easier for you to produce a response in the second language.

Even if you have a very limited vocabulary in the second language – maybe you know the colors, the numbers, some basic foods, basic articles of clothing – you can still ask questions to your child with one simple word. In Spanish that is "quieres." Q-U-I-E-R-E-S. You can say quieres and then say the two options. Quieres means, "Do you want?" Literally, you only need to say quieres and then the two options. I'll give you a quick example. Let's say that you have an apple and an orange, and you want to ask your child, "Do you want an apple or an orange?" and you want to do it in Spanish. Well, what if you don't know the word for apple or orange, but you know the colors. You could very easily say, "Do you want red or orange?" Let's say that you don't know the colors, but you know the number 1 and 2 in Spanish. Then you could say, "Do you want number 1?" and point to number 1, "Or do you want number 2?" and point to another fruit.

That is just a quick example of how you can use one word to connect it to the vocabulary that is inside of you probably from your high school or college Spanish class. With this just one word, you can create a lot of questions and actually give your child the vocabulary within the questions, so they can start producing.

Here's a quick video to help you further understand this concept

bilingualfamily.us/startsmall

In the following pages you will find common phrases and vocabulary you can use to develop your own routines.

Common Phrases

Me encanta – I love it.
Me gusta – I like it
¿Te gusta? – Do you like it?
Buenos días – Good morning
¿Cómo amaneciste? – How are you this morning? (How did you sleep?)
Ayúdame, por favor. – Help me please.
Dame un abrazo/beso. – Give me a hug/kiss.
Te quiero. – I love you.
Te amo. – I love you.
Dame la mano - Give me your hand
¿Éstas listo? - Are you ready?
¿Tienes hambre? – Are you hungry?
¿Quieres más? – Do you want more?
¿Acabaste/terminaste? – Are you done?
Por favor – Please
Gracias – Thank you
No gracias – No thank you
De nada – You're welcome

Necesitas Ayuda? - Do you need help?
¿Cuántos hay? – How many are there?
¡Mira! – Look.
Ven - Come here
¿Dónde estás? – Where are you?
Ten cuidado – Be careful.
Amárrate los zapatos – Tie your shoes
Ponte el/la/los/las_____ Put on _____
Cierra la puerta. – Close the door
Apaga la luz. – Turn off the light.
Buenas noches – Good night
Es hora de_(verb)___ - Time to _____
Es hora de ir a _(place)_____ - It's time to go to_____
Dónde está_el/la (noun)___ - Where is the_____
Quieres_(noun)_o_(noun)_____ - Do you want _____
Quieres _(verb)_____ - Do you want_____
Necesitamos_(noun/ verb) – We need_____
Vamos a _(place/ verb) - We are going to_____

Common Vebs	Common Foods
Comer — To Eat	Cereal - Cereal
Cantar — To Sing	Galletas — Crackers/Cookies
Dormir — To Sleep	Fruta - Fruit
Jugar — To play	Vegetales - Vegetables
Leer — To read	Leche - Milk
Escribir – To write	Agua — Water
Limpiar — To clean	Jugo - Juice
Salir — To leave/ go out	Jugo de____ -____Juice

Common Places	Common Things
La casa de ____- ____'s house	Jugetes - Toys
La tienda – The store	Bloques - Blocks
El supermercado – The supermarket	Carros - Cars
El parque – The park	Tren - Train
La escuela – The school	Peluches – Stuffed animals
La biblioteca – The library	Plastilina – Play-doh
El museo – The museum	Papel - Paper
La escuela – The school	Lapiz - Pencil
	Colores - Colors
	Pintura - Paint
	Legos - Legos
	Muñeca(o) – Doll/Action Figure
	Mochila – Backpack
	Lonchera – Lunch box

Family	Animals
Mamá - Mom	**Perro** – Dog
Papá - Dad	**Vaca** - Cow
Hermano - Brother	**Gato** – Cat
Hermana - Sister	**Caballo** - Horse
Abuelo/Abuelito - Grandma/ Grandpa	**Pez** – Fish
Abuela/Abuelita - Grandma/ Grandpa	**Cerdo** - Pig
Tio(a) – Uncle/Aunt	**Ratón** – Mouse
Primo(a) - Cousin	**Pollo** - Chicken
	Lagarto - Lizard
	Serpiente - Snake
	Conejo - Rabbit
	Tortuga - Turtle

Stories - Books

Even if you are in the early stages of your language-learning journey, you can learn from even the simplest of children's books. You can use the pictures as clues to help understand the content and build your vocabulary.

Surprisingly, parents who are learning a second language love children's books because they're non-threatening. They're easy, they have pictures and because they're with their children, parents don't feel like, "Oh my gosh, why am I reading a kid's book to learn Spanish." They are learning together. They're learning all these words together and it's not threatening, which makes it a low-stress activity for the children and for the parents. As Krashen[10] says, the biggest challenge with adults and learning a second language is you have to make the content comprehensible, but it also has to be interesting. If you're at a beginner level and you're an adult, there's not going to be much interesting stuff that's comprehensible. There's not going to be any books that are comprehensible and still interesting for adults. If you're reading with your child, it's interesting because you're spending quality time with your child and learning together.

REVIEW

If you stop at DO, your dream won't come true.

As your child grows and experiences the world, their interests and skills will change. For this reason, you must be prepared and willing to review your language plan regularly to meet their needs and keep their love for the language alive.

The best way to review is in real life situations and interactions with the community.

Some Ideas to Help You Review:

Online Resources:

Mama Lisa - Whether you are from Colombia, Mexico, Guatemala, or the U.S., chances are you have vivid childhood memories sparked by a song or rhyme from your native country.

---

10   Krashen, S. D. (1982). Principles and practice in second language acquisition. Oxford: Pergamon.

This resource will help you create new "cultural memories" with your child. Mama Lisa's World is a website where you can find the lyrics to kids' songs, in English and in the original languages from across the globe!

http://www.mamalisa.com/

Spanish Playground – This is a wonderful site full of activities, games, songs, books, songs, and so much more to help you and your child learn Spanish. The activities are designed to teach Spanish, but most can be used to teach any language.

* This site suggests some apps and online games. We believe that real and meaningful interactions are the best way to learn a second language.

http://www.spanishplayground.net/

Bilingual Family Resources:

Weekly Videos – Each week we release a video to help you raise bilingual children. The video topics include: Stages of Second Language Acquisition, Child Development, Guidance, How to... IN Spanish, children's songs, books, etc.

http://bilingualfamily.us/free-resources/

Recommended Books

We have a list of our favorite books for children and parents.

Routine PDFs - Download routine PDFs. We have the three different age groups (bebes 0-2 years, niños y niñas 3-5 years, y chicos y chicas 5+ years). The routines match each developmental stage, because the way you communicate with a baby is very different from the way you communicate with an 8-year-old. Also, we realize that if you are not a fluent Spanish speaker, you may not feel comfortable reading and pronouncing the vocabulary and phrases for these routines, so we have created an audio for each.

www.http://bilingualfamily.us/routines

Immersion Schools

Immersion schools are one of the best ways to find a community of like-minded parents. Some of the things to consider in choosing the best immersion schools for your family are the following:

- **Native teachers.** One of the main benefits of starting to learn the language at a young age is the accent. If children are exposed to native accents at an early age, they will more likely be able to produce the language without an accent. That is why native teachers are so important. Also, native teachers have a love for the language and the culture and are always very happy to share this love with families.

- **Knowledge:** It is crucial for the program and teachers to have an understanding of second-language acquisition and child development. As you now know, it is mandatory for you as a parent and anybody working with children to really have a strong understanding of how language is acquired and of child development. The founders and the teachers understand all the right ingredients to help your child become bilingual.

- **Support:** Be sure the programs support your journey. It is ideal for the immersion school to have programs which allow your child to be enrolled long-term. This is important for building relationships, as well as for the actual language acquisition. As you already know, language acquisition is a long journey. Being able to find a program that supports you through the journey is ideal.

- **Low teacher to student ratio.** Relationships are crucial in learning a second language, so it's important to have a really low teacher-to-student ratio. That way, each teacher will get to know your child and be able to individualize the language and the learning to his learning style.

- **Partnerships.** The program should see your relationship with the school as a partnership in helping your child become bilingual. When schools view families as partners and team members in the growth of the child and the education of the child, they will really create a powerful team for you.

Lunch/Coffee Friend

Find someone who is a speaker of the target language and develop a friendship with them. It's helpful to have a "lunch friend" and talk about things that interest you. Hopefully you have similar interests and you can develop a relationship, which is the most important aspect of learning a language.

The conversation is focused on building that relationship rather than correcting. When you are corrected, you feel frustrated and it blocks the language learning.

Community

Part of our mission is to create a community of bilingual families. We felt like we were on our way to doing so, but recently, I realized that we were already there, that we had already created a community of bilingual families.

I came to this realization at our art show. I overheard a conversation where a mom was explaining how she loved the fact that the majority of our families had at least one Spanish speaker at home. As I savored that comment, I started looking around and seeing all the families that were there. She was right. They either had one or two native speakers at home or they had a Spanish learner, someone who truly wanted to become a Spanish speaker, and it made me realize that a big part of the success of our students was created by this beautiful, dedicated, loving and intentional group of bilingual families.

The purpose of language is connection. Find or create a community where all the parents have the same goal of raising bilingual children. In order to really learn a second language, you need a community, a group of people who are also wanting to learn the language.

So now you have adopted the spirit of the teacher and understand the importance of relationships. You understand your child's development and the stages of Second Language Acquisition. You know that making language learning fun is mandatory, and you understand the power of repetition through the use of routines. Now you are ready to take on this journey.

Here's your challenge:

DREAM passionately
DO before you're ready
REVIEW constantly

DREAM, DO, REVIEW

Together we can create a community of bilingual families!

Made in the USA
San Bernardino, CA
04 February 2017